ENDORSEMENTS

Cady, who married my son Jordan in o
fearless faith and boundless love to a jour ... uian
we thought, but brought us all closer to our merciful Father. This gift of
a book will breathe life-giving hope to all who read it.

—RON LEWIS
Sr. Minister, Every Nation Church NYC

Her Grief Was Heard: Diary from a Young Widow's Heart is a must read for
those journeying through the heartbreak of significant loss. The story
of Cady and Jordan is one of the most poignant and heart-wrenching I
have ever encountered in over forty years of ministry. Never have I seen
the courage displayed by Cady as first a wife and then a young widow.
In this book she takes us behind the scenes and behind the veil of public
images allowing us to experience the out-of-sight moments when only
God could have brought her through. Out of deep pain comes significant
ministry, and this book will minister to you significantly. I am so proud
of Cady and of our Lord for his amazing grace in her life!

—DR. WILLIAM M. WILSON
President, Oral Roberts University

Processing grief is one of the most challenging and essential tasks in the
Christian life. In *Her Grief Was Heard*, Cady Patterson takes us with her
through her own experience of devastating loss into the light of hope
and healing. For those who have lost their way in the pain of grief and
unexpected loss, read this book and let Cady's journey be a beacon of light
to your own.

—JOHN CARTER
Pastor, Abundant Life
Syracuse, NY

With great courage and transparency, Cady Patterson has relived her season of deepest pain and loss through *Her Grief was Heard*. When Christians experience such loss, the overwhelming darkness of grief launches unrelenting attacks on personal faith while crushing the survivor with guilt and devastating emotions and questions. Cady's journey provides a healing ointment that brings comfort, healing, insight, and the discovery of a new self that can stand up and face the future with genuine hope through Jesus Christ.

—BISHOP LADONNA OSBORN, D.MIN.
President, Osborn Ministries International
Presiding Bishop, International Gospel Fellowship of
Churches and Ministries

HER GRIEF WAS HEARD

HER GRIEF WAS HEARD

CADY PATTERSON

BRIDGE LOGOS

Newberry, FL 32669

Bridge-Logos

Newberry, FL 32669

Her Grief Was Heard

by Cady Patterson

Copyright © 2019 by Bridge-Logos

Printed in the United States of America

Library of Congress Catalog Card Number: 2019932108

International Standard Book Number: 978-1-61036-404-1

Unless otherwise indicated, Scripture quotations are from the Holy Bible, English Standard Version. ESV® Text Edition: 2016. Copyright © 2001 by Crossway Bibles, a publishing ministry of Good News Publishers.

Edited by Lynn Copeland

Cover design, photo credit by Sarah Bridgeman | sarahbridgemancreative.com

Interior design by Kent Jensen | knail.com

CONTENTS

FOREWORD

It was a nightmare, a horrible dream, and we were in it together—Cady and me and a host of other warriors fighting for the win, a healing, any sort of breakthrough to keep our son Jordan alive.

When he died, and our hearts and dreams were broken, we were thrust into chapters of our stories we never would have written.

Cady, our darling daughter-in-law, lived with us for the first six months, and in many ways became my grief partner and grief coach. We talked till the wee morning hours, laughing over some of the memories of our beloved Jordan and crying over others. Watching her navigate the uncharted highs and lows, questions and wrestlings, was a gift beyond what I knew then.

Five years later and so deeply bonded still, I picked up these words of truth and wisdom in *Her Grief Was Heard* and marvel at how God faithfully brought beauty out of ashes. Cady masterfully describes the journey and points our gaze to the only One who can ultimately make sense out of such pain.

Whatever you're facing you will find on these pages a heart yielded, and thus transformed, by the God of all hope who comforts like no other. May He likewise bring you this hope that heals.

LYNETTE LEWIS, Jordan's stepmom
Author, TEDx Speaker, Pastor's Wife

ACKNOWLEDGMENTS

I have many people to thank for this opportunity, but first and foremost I would like to thank my Saving King, Jesus Christ, who redeemed my brokenness and rescued me from darkness and brought me into the Father's marvelous light. Thank you, Jesus, for collecting every one of my tears and breathing joy back into my being. I am in complete awe of you.

My sweet husband, Jonathan Ezell Patterson, you carried this book with me from the very beginning. Your pursuit of my heart and my dreams never ceases to amaze and humble me. You have shown me the love of Christ in ways I will never be able to express this side of heaven. You have made countless silent sacrifices so that this dream of mine could be a reality. Thank you. Your gentleness, strength, bravery, and wisdom that I've always admired showed truer than ever through your loving support during my hours of writing, processing, tear-shedding, and celebrating. Thank you for the late-night proofreads, the encouraging pep talks, and being my number one support system through this entire writing journey. I will never be able to put into words how much your encouragement and support has impacted me.

Mom, you are stinkin' awesome and I love you. I know you felt my suffering in ways I will never understand. I am really proud to be your daughter. You are my role model of what it means to be a woman. I treasure your strength and bravery.

Dad, thank you for being the first to "Google" my book, and for all the sweet texts and phone calls to encourage me on this journey. You're the best.

Kim, thank you for praying countless hours through late nights and early mornings for me as I wrote this book. Even in the midst of being a full-time caretaker yourself, you relentlessly interceded for this book and covered me in prayer.

Lewis, I am so thankful for our "big ol' happy family" and I have you to thank for the "happy" part with the barrels of laughs you always provide!

Claire, thank you for your attention to detail. And Christian, thank you for marrying her! Love you, brother.

Jessey, you have been my big sister from the beginning. Thank you for always being in my corner—through tears and sunshine.

I will always be eternally grateful and have the utmost respect for Suzi Wooldridge and the way she diligently serves the Lord through Bridge-Logos Publishing—thank you for this humbling opportunity.

Mrs. Carol, thank you for believing in me and being an answer to a prayer in a season of dreaming.

Ron and Lynette, thank you for encouraging me through this journey with your love and empowerment—it has been such a gift to me. I have been deeply humbled by your support.

My editor, Lynn, you have been such a joy to work with, and I appreciate you understanding my writing voice as well as my heart for this book.

Sarah, thank you for this beautiful cover!

INTRODUCTION

At age twenty-four I became a newlywed...and a widow. I married my college sweetheart, Jordan, three weeks after he was diagnosed with stage IV sinus cancer. We discovered this news when he returned from a missions trip to Tanzania, where his team had built a birthing center for mothers. Jordan had nose bleeds so severe he was bleeding through his eyes. The next eight and a half months of our short marriage became the most traumatic experience of my life. And I am the type of girl who hasn't even seen the movie *Bambi* in its entirety, because I get too emotional after Bambi's mother dies. There were so many times I asked God why I had to witness such a grueling death of my husband, knowing how sensitive He created me.

The type of cancer was gruesome and completely took over my groom's body—but not once did Jordan blame God for his suffering. We believed that Jordan was going to be healed from cancer. In fact, I even prayed over his lifeless body after he breathed his last breath. But this was not the plan God had for our lives. When Jordan started to experience labored breathing, the nurse let me know that I was holding him for the last time. I fell on my knees on that hospital floor and asked God to spare my heart from bitterness and to guard my heart from becoming hard. Guess what? The Lord was faithful and fulfilled my prayer.

This book is a collection of journal entries I wrote during my journey through grief. Every Scripture nestled in these pages comforted my heart as I sifted through the trauma I experienced. After Jordan died, I read C. S. Lewis' *A Grief Observed*, and it changed my life. Lewis had lost his wife to cancer and he vulnerably wrestles with his faith as he grieves the life of his beloved. It was the first book that validated my feelings and didn't tiptoe around the raw and ugly feelings of grief.

I wrote this book because I needed it when I was wrestling through faith questions and struggling with heartache so intense I felt like I couldn't breathe. This devotional is the book I desperately wanted during my time of grief. But I can tell you, dear reader, that every promise from Scripture, every nugget of hope and encouragement written in God's Word, pulled me out of the trenches of despair and brought me into a place of healing and restoration—a place of hope.

The chapters of this devotional are titled with very real, and very raw, feelings I had as I was walking through my grief. My prayer is that if you feel too weak to even get out of bed in the morning, you can roll over and grab this book from your nightstand and turn to "The Pain of Waking Up" entry and be comforted by a Bible verse that got me out of bed when I was feeling depressed. I know that when grieving, it's overwhelming to even open a book sometimes. I wrote this devotional to be as easily accessible for you as possible. If there is a feeling you have felt, there is probably an entry with that title.

No matter what you have seen, heard, or experienced, I want you to know one truth during your season of grief: God is near you, and only in Him is there hope. Remember it is a season; it will not be like this forever. Despite what you are feeling in the depths of the grief cycle, know that God sees you and knows your pain, and in His Word there is a God-breathed Scripture for everything you encounter. He is the first to your side, and last one singing over you before you fall asleep. This too shall pass.

Graveside Memorial Service

I never thought I would be sitting here in front of a box that is holding my husband's lifeless body. People are weeping, sharing their memories, touching his casket. This is all so strange. Just yesterday I was talking to him; I was holding his hand! Now I am starting to grasp the hard truth that I will never hold Jordan's hand again.

Is this how your disciples felt, when you were publicly mocked and crucified? The hope of the world, suffering and suffocating while they sheepishly hid in fear for their own lives. They had no idea what would happen in three days. But we know that your crucifixion wasn't the end of the story—it was only the beginning.

> But the angel said to the women, "Do not be afraid, for I know that you seek Jesus who was crucified. He is not here, for he has risen, as he said. Come, see the place where he lay." (Matthew 28:5,6)

It is because you were not in the tomb that we have eternal hope. Jordan's casket contains his physical body, but nothing else. You changed history for me over two thousand years ago. Because your tomb is empty my heart is full. I can hold on to the hope that that is not the end, and this is not forever. Until we meet again, I will hold on to your promises.

I am strangely comforted even while standing over his grave, because deep down in my heart I know Jordan isn't here. He is with you, whole and free from all pain. As friends and family are walking by his casket, I feel empty and numb; but I know the truth. Jordan's story doesn't end here, at the soil beneath my feet. His life has just begun with the Creator who intricately knows and loves him. Tears are now running down my cheeks at the thought of Jordan finally being able to behold your glory, running on two strong legs at full speed into your open arms.

And though I am sitting alone beside Jordan's empty body I feel your sweet voice whispering promises of hope and love into my heart. I will be reunited with you one day and this emptiness I feel now will be nothing but a memory.

My soul rests in knowing that gladness and joy is for me because I will one day be reunited with you—the one who paid my ransom with your own life. My hope doesn't cease if I don't receive a healing miracle. My hope doesn't fade when I bury my spouse and close the casket.

And I heard a loud voice from the throne saying, "Behold, the dwelling place of God is with man. He will dwell with them, and they will be his people, and God himself will be with them as their God. He will wipe away every tear from their eyes, and death shall be no more, neither shall there be mourning, nor crying, nor pain anymore, for the former things have passed away." (Revelation 21:3,4)

Starting Over

I looked back at the life I just left behind. Wow. The amount of life I experienced in such a short span of time makes me feel like I have lived a thousand years in less than nine months. I feel like I am fifty years older, and that I have been grieving for at least two decades. I know that life is not over for me. You are not finished with me yet. But it still feels so odd to be starting over.

I don't know exactly what life is supposed to look like now. I don't know what my new normal should be. I have different accomplishments and different hurdles every day. I know I have a new and different life ahead of me and it terrifies me. I'm not sure whether to plunge forward or pull back in caution. I have learned to let go and be fearless, but I have also felt like I have been stretching my hand out to test the waters, only to pull it back quickly, like a child being slapped on the hand.

My thought life is plagued with flashbacks of sweet memories and of painful ones, things I wish I never said and things I wish I said more. I have noticed that every time I go down this dangerous path of what-ifs, you silently step into my thought-life and remind me that I am looking at this through the wrong set of lenses. There is so much more you are doing in my life than what I am focusing on. There are more mountains to climb, more adventures for me to pursue, and more friendships for me to cherish. You shift my gaze from the brokenness to hopefulness, and this helps me redefine what my new life should look like.

My hope shines all the more brightly through the stormy days of grief because I know that this sorrow isn't the unhappy ending to my story. Hope is the one thing Christians have that makes us different from everyone else who is grieving. Hope reminds us that this is not the end, but only the beginning. My grief is but a thread in the grand tapestry you are weaving; each phase of my life is a thread of vibrant color, intricately woven together to create a beautiful masterpiece. One day I will stand back and behold the tapestry, seeing that not one thread of my life was wasted, but all were used by your hands to make something beautiful.

When I am struggling with knowing your plans, when I feel downtrodden by the world around me, I can look to you and cry out for help. This journey of starting over will happen only if I am leaning on your guidance.

Even if all I can utter to you today is, "Help me!" you will hear me. It is enough for you.

Every now and then I feel like you give me a peek of the entire piece you are intricately weaving with your fingers, showing me that there is so much more that you are doing in my life than I could imagine. You give me glimpses of your beautiful handiwork, stirring my faith and filling my eyes with hope.

Therefore, if anyone is in Christ, he is a new creation. The old has passed away; behold, the new has come. (2 Corinthians 5:17)

I Am Feeling Overwhelmed

There is so much to do. Just because the memorial service is over doesn't mean the endless list of all I need to get done is completed. Along with my lengthy to-do list, I have to figure out what I am going to do with the rest of my life.

There are hospital bills stacked high on my kitchen counter. There is a lease renewal for the apartment to sign, a new home to find, and boxes and boxes of Jordan's belongings I need to go through. I think it is safe to say that I am overwhelmed. And that's not even the worst part; the worst part of it all is that my husband is dead.

> *If the LORD had not been my help, my soul would soon have lived in the land of silence.*　　　　　　　　　　　　　　　　(Psalm 94:17)

You got me through the past week. You held my hand as I went through Jordan's clothes. They still smelled like him. You walked beside me when I picked out his burial place. "Oh wow, you're young!" they'd say. *So was Jordan,* I'd think to myself. When I was choosing the songs, the details, the pictures, I could feel the warmth of your voice whispering to me, "I'm going to get you through this."

If I didn't have you, I do not know where I would be.

> *When I thought, "My foot slips," your steadfast love, O LORD, held me up.*　　　　　　　　　　　　　　　　(Psalm 94:18)

This past week, I walked through something I never thought I could walk through. But of one thing I am certain: I need you.

> *When the cares of my heart are many, your consolations cheer my soul.*　　　　　　　　　　　　　　　　(Psalm 94:19)

I know that when I tackle the ambulance bills tomorrow, you will sustain me. When I finally get around to opening that one box that has every sentimental thing ever owned by Jordan, you will hold my heart.

I will take one step at a time. Whenever I start to feel overwhelmed, I will look to you and you will get me through the next step.

Honestly, it gives me great peace knowing that my life is not one big surprise party for you. Because it sure has felt like a never-ending surprise party for me. (Only not the fun kind of party—the kind of party with no balloons or cake, just boxes, bills, and lots of crying.)

You already know what I am feeling, and this encourages me. At least one of us knows what I am feeling and why I am feeling it. I will lean on you because you already have this all figured out. I will rest in your presence knowing that you have already gone before me. Tomorrow, we will tackle my humongous to-do list. You will be right by my side every step of the way.

I Feel So Alone

It was finally date night. Jordan was in the middle of his rounds with chemotherapy and feeling pretty sick, so we decided to make date night a stay-at-home venture with rented movies and a picnic in the living room. I set up a cozy picnic with blankets and pillows, along with Jordan's favorite Chinese takeout food. We were determined to make the best of the night, regardless of the grueling side effects of chemotherapy. I still dressed up for the date and wore a cute new white dress for the occasion, since I considered myself a new bride almost eight weeks into our marriage.

Suddenly, all hell broke loose. Out of nowhere, Jordan's nose started bleeding uncontrollably. Blood rimmed his eyes, and he started to get lightheaded from the loss of so much blood. I raced to get our routine emergency nosebleed supplies: fluids, rags and tissues, and a chair. Jordan tilted his head back to slow the bleeding, but it was so much blood he started to choke as it drained back into his throat. He quickly threw his head forward causing blood to spill everywhere. I still remember the sound: like a full cup of water poured onto bathroom tile.

I finally got the bleeding under control, cleaned up Jordan's face and clothes, and gave him fluid to rehydrate. I got him all tucked in comfortably in the living room and told him I would be right there after I used the restroom. After making sure he was comfortable and content, I closed the bathroom door and turned toward the mirror: I was covered in blood. My new white sundress was damp with bright red splotches of my sweet husband's blood. I gasped and turned on the water faucet to cover my sobs; I was not going to let my sadness ruin our date night.

Lord, I was so afraid. I knew that this was only the beginning of the journey ahead of us—and I was absolutely terrified. I had no idea how I was going to stay strong.

But I will never forget what you said to me that night in the bathroom. As I washed Jordan's blood off of my face, hands, and dress I cried to you: "Do you see me, God? Do you know my pain?"

In that moment, you reminded me of your mother, Mary, sitting at the feet of the cross where you hung. I imagine her looking up at you, her precious Son, feeling absolutely helpless and in utter despair. Your blood is on her face and hands, for she has reached up to touch your feet in a feeble attempt to comfort her Son. In the agony of your suffering, you see every face of every sinner you will call into your marvelous light. And in the sea of faces, you see mine. Though you are suffering from the weight of my sin, you see me. You know my pain.

You saw that moment, where I was trying to sneakily cry in my bathroom on date night, so my husband wouldn't hear me and be sad. Yes, you saw me, and you knew exactly how I felt.

Today I am struggling with feeling lonely. I mean, being a full-time caretaker at age twenty-three is a pretty narrow demographic. Does anyone understand my fears and sadness? You do. The same God who was with me in the bathroom, comforting a newlywed bride in her utter despair, is the same God who understands my pain more than I do. You were with me then, and you are with me now. In my loneliness, I will do the only thing I know I can: I will cry out to you. I will offer all of my trauma and woes to you, placing my burdens at your feet. I am moved to worship you and trust your goodness, because you are the only one who sees me in this moment and you are the only one who knows exactly how I feel. I wasn't alone when I was caretaking for Jordan then, and I am not alone as a twenty-four-year-old widow now.

"For the waves of death encompassed me, the torrents of destruction assailed me; the cords of Sheol entangled me; the snares of death confronted me. In my distress I called upon the LORD; to my God I called. From his temple he heard my voice, and my cry came to his ears." (2 Samuel 22:5–7)

The First Time I Went to Church by Myself

This morning I went to church for the first time since Jordan died. I masterfully avoided the "meet-and-greet" time of the service. I strategically exited the church through the side door to avoid awkward lobby conversations. During the service, I sat by myself in our usual section. Okay, note to self: that was a dumb idea. Find a new section to sit in next Sunday. That experience was way too painful.

So many holy moments flooded my mind during the church service. I remember the times Jordan would put his arm around me during the message. It was always so special when we would take communion together. Now, I sit by myself and it is really hard not to notice all the couples sitting all around me. Goodness, is today Happily Married Couples' Day at church or something?

But this is the body of Christ you have given to me. I can go to church with tears and worship with other believers who also have battle scars like I do. You nestled me into this home away from home, and this morning I get to worship with the saints in unison declaring that you are good and faithful.

I look around my church and see the faces of the saints, each representing a story, a journey that somehow your hand has touched. Some of these stories have pages that are stained with tears, some are laced with substance abuse and addiction, others have pages that are still waiting for their happy ending. We all have one thing in common: we need our Savior. You are the author of our stories. We all have twisted backgrounds and sinful downfalls. But you call us into the grand masterpiece you are writing to operate as one body.

These are the people who prayed for me and did fundraisers to help support me. This body of Christ stood around me when I was too weak to stand on my own. Sure, they may not know the right things to say at this season of my life, but they are also processing losing a loved one from their church family.

I may be sitting by myself in church today, but I am surrounded by my brothers and sisters you have given to me by your grace.

But our citizenship is in heaven, and from it we await a Savior, the Lord Jesus Christ. (Philippians 3:20)

Likewise, my brothers, you also have died to the law through the body of Christ, so that you may belong to another, to him who has been raised from the dead, in order that we may bear fruit for God. (Romans 7:4)

Where Are You?

There are many moments throughout the day when I feel like my mind sounds like a broken record. I keep repeating the same things, reliving the same memories, and crying the same tears. I feel like I am constantly processing my new life as a widow and the old life I had as a bride. I am always trying to fight back the tears that are on the brink of spilling over onto my cheeks. Will there ever be a moment of relief from this?

I know you are not a King who merely watches your people suffer and struggle. I know you are not passive. You could be if you wanted to, but in your relentless grace and abounding glory you are a rescuer who steps down from the heavens to redeem the brokenness of your people.

As strange as it sounds, when I look back at the days in the hospital or the days I felt the lowest in my journey of grief, I can always see moments where you made yourself so tangible to me through your comfort. When I think back at that moment in the hospital room when I was told Jordan would breathe his last breath, I see you there, your hand on my back, comforting me.

You are more than just a comforting hand. In all your righteousness and sovereignty, you owe me nothing but gave me everything. You gave me that precious season with Jordan. And now as I battle my thoughts of sorrow, you recklessly break into my thought life, fighting for me and proclaiming your promises over me. You remind me that you are near and that I am tucked under your wings. You whisper your comforting promises to me and I get an overwhelming sense that I am never alone. My heart doesn't always tell the truth, but your Scriptures always do.

The LORD is near to all who call on him, to all who call on him in truth. He fulfills the desire of those who fear him; he also hears their cry and saves them. (Psalm 145:18,19)

Let me dwell in your tent forever! Let me take refuge under the shelter of your wings! (Psalm 61:4)

I Am at a Loss for Words

I am sitting alone in my living room in complete silence. I have nothing to say. My heart feels hollow and empty, like a dark tomb. I have cried all my tears and sifted every memory of Jordan. I feel heavy, as if this pain I have been carrying for so long has drained my heart of all hope.

> O LORD, how many are my foes! Many are rising against me; many are saying of my soul, "There is no salvation for him in God." Selah
>
> But you, O LORD, are a shield about me, my glory, and the lifter of my head. I cried aloud to the LORD, and he answered me from his holy hill.
>
> (Psalm 3:1–4)

I feel like my voice has been silenced by the waves of grief. I am at a loss for words. I do not even know how I should pray or what I should pray for.

> Likewise the Spirit helps us in our weakness. For we do not know what to pray for as we ought, but the Spirit himself intercedes for us with groanings too deep for words. And he who searches hearts knows what is the mind of the Spirit, because the Spirit intercedes for the saints according to the will of God.
>
> (Romans 8:26,27)

In my loss for words, you will intercede on my behalf. When I am unable to articulate the chambers of my heart's troubles, you will intercede for me with groanings too deep for words. You have searched my heart and you know the depths of my troubles; you know me better than I know myself. You will take up my cause and carry it for me, interceding for me when I am without words.

You help me in my weakness, even if I am praying for the wrong thing, or not even knowing what I should pray. You know my weaknesses, but you do not leave me here alone. You have lifted my head at the promise that you are my shield in times of trouble. The whole world could be rising up against me, yet you would rescue me from it all.

Someone Just Told Me God Is Good...and I Don't Believe It

I had an interesting little encounter today. While I was at the gym, an acquaintance came up to me who knew that I had just lost Jordan. She politely asked how I was doing, and what I was up to these days. I was honest with her—I mean, I am the one learning to live without a husband, no use in sugar-coating the situation—and then, she did it. She dropped that four-worded response that makes my skin crawl. I told her I missed Jordan and how sad I was for the pain he endured. She looked at me and quickly responded with, "Well, God is good," and hurriedly headed toward the treadmills. Thanks for nothing, sister. Did you even hear what I just said?

These days, I have a mind full of questions I ask you daily. Sometimes I get angry with you. Sometimes I ask you questions that could make a person cringe (even myself!). But after every single time we have a colorful conversation, I feel more loved than I did before—even with my fists shaking at the heavens while I am yelling to you, *"Why?!"*

When I look at the Psalms or read about Job in the Bible, I am always amazed at the fantastic emotional one-liners. Those are raw feelings right there. No sugar-coated, "Hello, God, I feel as if I am currently experiencing a bit of angst because this situation is rather challenging." Nope. I can actually relate to these people.

When someone tells me, "Well, God is good" as a response to my suffering, I feel like it is such a copout. I do not need anybody telling me just how good you are. I also know you don't need anyone else justifying your goodness either. You speak for yourself. You show me your goodness through your tenderness in my fragile state. When I am angry or confused by your character, you gently sing over me, patiently consoling my careless accusations.

The Bible shares examples of those who love God but speak their minds in the midst of their grief. They are saying things that I have not only thought to myself, but I have actually said out loud to you too. However, it is in these moments of questioning your goodness that I experience the depths of your lovingkindness. You loved me before I even knew you existed. You have been carrying me through my real-life nightmare, and now I am yelling at you while you carry me over the shifting seas. I am reminded that you have felt what I am feeling, only deeper. Yet I speak to you with clenched teeth, hoping to make you flinch. But you hold me even closer. I know what I have read about you: tattered body, barely breathing, you lifted your sweet head to cry through your bloody lips, "My God, my God, why have you forsaken me?"

You know me, and you know my pain more deeply than I do. My tears have been counted, and my prayers have been heard. It may sound cliché—after all, we say this to everyone who has ever experienced grief. But it sounds the best from the one who is listening.

I am determined to set my hopes on what you will do with my tears. My hope is in the fact that one day you will wipe away every tear I have shed. Though I do not see the light at the end of the tunnel right now, I know one thing: you are standing here with me in my darkest of days. You have my name on the palms of your hands.

And at the ninth hour Jesus cried with a loud voice, "Eloi, Eloi, lema sabachthani?" which means, "My God, my God, why have you forsaken me?" (Mark 15:34)

"Behold, I have engraved you on the palms of my hands; your walls are continually before me." (Isaiah 49:16)

Tonight I Cannot Sleep

This is one of those nights. It is a little past three in the morning, and I'm lying in the dark in my obnoxiously oversized bed that used to have two inhabitants. I tried moving to the middle of the mattress to make a "pillow nest" around me so I wouldn't feel as alone, but it didn't work. I am crying too hard to fall asleep anyway. The grueling images of Jordan suffering physical pain are seared on the backs of my eyelids. The reality of being awake makes my heart ache but closing my eyes to escape the agony is like walking through the mouth of a dark cave filled with all of my most painful memories. I don't want to fall asleep because I fear I will have that same nightmare once again, the one where Jordan is dying and deteriorating in front of me and there is nothing I can do to stop it.

Even if I sleep without dreams, I will wake only to rediscover that I am here alone, and yes, my husband really did die, and no, he will never come back again.

So, here I am, Lord. I turned on the lights and I am sitting up at this point because my tears were rolling down into my ears. I just want this sorrow to leave me. Will I always feel like this?

I cried aloud to the Lord, and he answered me from his holy hill. I lay down and slept; I woke again, for the Lord sustained me. (Psalm 3:4,5)

My only hope at this point is to cry out to you. And somehow, I am comforted by this. I have nothing left in me but to cry out to you. Lord, am I too broken to piece back together? I feel as if you aren't even worried about that part. You just want me.

In peace I will both lie down and sleep; for you alone, O Lord, make me dwell in safety. (Psalm 4:8)

You are the only one who sees every second of every sleepless hour, and somehow you sustain me. You do not try to hush me like a misbehaving toddler or avert my attention to distract me from my heartache. No, you run to my bedside in the early hours of the night and sing over me with your love. You are not ashamed of my brokenness. Your hand is on my face, collecting each tear that rolls down my chapped cheeks. I may wake in the night remembering the weighted burden of my loss, but you will sustain me.

When I tried to suffocate my sobs under pillows and sheets, you held my head to your chest and wept with me. When I toss and turn in the untimely hours of the night, your hand is on my back, whispering words of comfort over me. Through piles of tissues and stacks of old wedding photos, you cherish every memory with me and tenderly grieve my loss with me.

Tonight, I know in my head that you haven't forgotten me, even though I may not be feeling that truth in my heart. However, I know that I am not left to the vices of my own disdain. And even though no one shares the pillows and sheets with me tonight, I do know one thing: I am not alone.

The Pain of Waking Up

This morning I woke up and felt like a ton of bricks were piled on my chest. The burden of my loss is physically heavy at times, especially this morning. I lift my hands to my face to rub my eyes as they adjust to the morning light. My cheeks are damp. I must have been crying while I was asleep again. I remember when the mornings were sweet and refreshing to my soul. Now it seems that when I wake, it is all that I can muster within me to get out of bed and take a shower.

Oh, to have that first moment of breathing in the fresh morning air be sweet again! The first breath of waking-up bliss, sleepily blinking awake, trying to recollect yourself, remembering where you are, what day it is, and then... oh, right. My loved one is dead. The harsh reality floods back into my mind, abruptly reminding me of the heartache I almost forgot, and that no matter how many birds are chirping outside, or how warm the sun's rays are, my reality is a cold, harsh, and very lonely one. For one second, I forgot that I am a widow, but was harshly reminded by the warmth of the morning sun peering through my blinds that this truth is just as real as the sun that is shining. Remembering it all over again is even more painful.

I won't hear the water running in the bathroom while Jordan shaves his face. Why was I always so annoyed when he would bang around too loudly in the morning? I'd do anything to be startled awake by him accidentally slamming the door or dropping breakfast utensils in the kitchen.

When I wake up the nightmare begins.

When I wake your mercy steps in.

The steadfast love of the LORD never ceases; his mercies never come to an end; they are new every morning; great is your faithfulness. "The LORD is my portion," says my soul, "therefore I will hope in him."

(Lamentations 3:22–24)

When I wake, I may be flooded with memories of sadness. But there is something else greeting me every morning before my feet hit the floor.

Your mercy is standing in my doorway as soon as my eyes open. It leaps to my bedside when my head doesn't want to come off of the pillow. When the moment comes that I remember my heartache, your mercy rushes to my side, your hand on my back reminding me that today is a new day. Your mercy meets me where I am, gently taking hold of my hands and showing me that you will always be here for me. Your mercy is gentle, yet it is fierce. And when tomorrow morning comes, and I don't want to wake up again, you will be waiting for me bedside, your eyes faithfully fixed on giving me a new day of hope. And in this painful new way of waking up, I know I can collapse into your arms, every single morning until I am strong enough to stand on my own.

Knowing that your mercies are never ending is of great comfort to me, because I am so painfully aware that people do not last forever. But your love does.

Weeping may tarry for the night, but joy comes with the morning.
(Psalm 30:5)

Did You Abandon Me?

Where were you when the doctor said there was nothing he could do to help Jordan? Were you there when Jordan's eyesight faded and when he collapsed on the ground in pain? Were you there when I cried myself to sleep, silently lying next to a sick and dying husband?

> *Awake! Why are you sleeping, O Lord? Rouse yourself! Do not reject us forever! Why do you hide your face? Why do you forget our affliction and oppression? For our soul is bowed down to the dust; our belly clings to the ground. Rise up; come to our help! Redeem us for the sake of your steadfast love!* (Psalm 44:23–26)

I cried out to you in my total despair. Like the psalmist, my prayers were desperate. But in the darkest of my nights, you came running to me.

> *Rejoice greatly, O daughter of Zion! Shout aloud, O daughter of Jerusalem! Behold, your king is coming to you; righteous and having salvation is he, humble and mounted on a donkey, on a colt, the foal of a donkey.* (Zechariah 9:9)

You came to my rescue. You never once abandoned me. You were holding Jordan when he first heard the news that the cancer was back. You were the hand on Jordan's back as we frantically searched for tissues for another severe nosebleed. You were the one sitting right beside me whispering your promises of faithfulness, when the doctors were stating their limitations. You were the one collecting every tear that fell from my eyes when I was sobbing alone in the hospital waiting room.

You were always there. This is the comfort that keeps me sane right now—the comforting fact knowing that you walked this entire journey with me. You are walking with me now, even though I feel abandoned. I know that is just a lie. When I look back I can see you in every moment of my journey. I see your hand on the gracious nurses who tenderly loved and cared for Jordan. I see your hand in the community that stood with me and prayed for Jordan's healing. I see you sitting here at my kitchen table while I am wondering how I am supposed to pay these bills.

I know you are with me and I know you will never abandon me.

Will the Crying Ever Stop?

I'm always so moved by the word "ransomed" when I see it in Scripture. A payment was demanded for my release from my own chains. Each link I bear from my own doing, separating me from my King. Yet I never had to pay this price, this ransom, to which I was indebted for my life. I owed a huge debt and never had to pay it—but my Savior did.

> *And the ransomed of the LORD shall return and come to Zion with singing; everlasting joy shall be upon their heads…* (Isaiah 35:10)

You loved me sacrificially. You paid the self-inflicted ransom that warranted my life and replaced my debts with a song to sing and a crown of everlasting joy.

I think of every tear I have shed on this side of heaven. Sometimes my face cramps from crying so hard. Yet I know every single tear has been bought by Christ. I know this sadness in my heart will not last forever.

My battle cry is my song of worship that I will sing to you. Through silent pleas for Jordan to come back, to heartbroken sobs from missing him, I will sing my heart out to you. I know I can come to you with the pieces of my heart because I know that you will hear me.

> *…they shall obtain gladness and joy, and sorrow and sighing shall flee away.* (Isaiah 35:10)

I know that there will be a day when my smeared mascara and puffy eyes will only be a memory. I know that I will laugh again—and not just any kind of laughter, but the kind of laughter that rolls from deep within the gut, full of exploding joy! I will be restored. This season of tears is simply a season. It will not last forever.

> *He will swallow up death forever; and the Lord GOD will wipe away tears from all faces, and the reproach of his people he will take away from all the earth, for the LORD has spoken.*

It will be said on that day, "Behold, this is our God; we have waited for him, that he might save us. This is the LORD; we have waited for him; let us be glad and rejoice in his salvation." (Isaiah 25:8,9, ESV)

The First Time I Went to His Grave Since the Memorial Service

I went to the place where I buried Jordan for the first time today since his memorial service. My stomach was in knots as I walked down the sidewalk to his stone. Oddly, I felt a little frightened and nervous. It's such an odd concept to know the body I knew and adored is now beneath soil. I honestly thought I would lose it when I saw his name on the headstone, and the mound of soil over his bones, the bones I loved.

> Behold! I tell you a mystery. We shall not all sleep, but we shall all be changed, in a moment, in the twinkling of an eye, at the last trumpet. For the trumpet will sound, and the dead will be raised imperishable, and we shall be changed. For this perishable body must put on the imperishable, and this mortal body must put on immortality. When the perishable puts on the imperishable, and the mortal puts on immortality, then shall come to pass the saying that is written: "Death is swallowed up in victory."
>
> (1 Corinthians 15:51–54)

My soul still aches from my loss, but my heart knows the truth. The mystery of this journey is how the most painful thing I have ever endured is simultaneously tangled up in an undeniable hope. I grieve that I am standing over this pile of earth which separates me from my husband's body, but I delight in the hope of knowing that Jordan isn't really here, but he is reunited with you. My everlasting hope is in the one who has carried me through the dark tumultuous waters of grief while freely running hand-in-hand through the rolling fields of heaven with Jordan.

My everlasting hope is in the fact that I will be reunited with you one day. Though I grieve, I have hope, a hope you breathed into my broken heart. It is this hope that keeps me going, until I am reunited with you. And to that I say:

O death, where is your victory?
O death, where is your sting?

I Feel Lonely

I would like to say that today is easier. I would like to say that today I am happier. But I would be lying to myself if I claimed this was true. So, I won't. Today I am still so very sad and I cannot remember the last time I felt deeply happy.

I tore at the walls and screamed out your name, "My God, why have you done this to me?" You stood in the room and stood by my side, not flinching at my words, or wincing at my anger. You were there. You never left me.

Is it strange to say the closest I have felt to heaven was the day Jordan died? As he took his last breath here on earth, I felt your hand on my back, and in that moment, I knew that I may feel lonely in this life, but I will never be alone. As Jordan slipped out of this life and into your arms, I felt half of myself break off from me and enter into heaven. It's strange to say the darkest day of my life has a beacon of hope shining through it. The night he died I cried and screamed, I threw things and wailed. But deep down in my heart, I knew you were in that hospital room with me. I knew you would never leave me.

When I look back at the past months without Jordan, I can see that you were with me through every "first" without him. You never left me.

You sang over me the first night I slept in our bed alone. You held me on his first birthday I had without him.

Though I felt abandoned in a world of emptiness, you were still there. Though I had no hand to hold when I was afraid, you never let me go.

Though I experienced a lot of "firsts," I will never experience a "last" of you holding me.

Draw near to God, and he will draw near to you.   (James 4:8)

At my first defense no one came to stand by me, but all deserted me. May it not be charged against them! But the Lord stood by me and strengthened me, so that through me the message might be fully proclaimed and all the Gentiles might hear it. So I was rescued from the lion's mouth.

(2 Timothy 4:16,17)

Will I Ever Be My Old Self Again?

Grief has been such a strange experience. It feels as if my mind has been severed from itself. Normal things, such as reading a book or having a casual conversation with another person, are difficult for me. Activities I once loved to do are now of little to no interest to me. I feel like my mind is constantly processing my loss while still trying to function through my regular daily routine. A lot of times I feel like half of my mind is in one place while the other half is thinking of Jordan.

Normal things are so difficult for me to wrap my mind around. Sometimes I don't remember little things I did throughout the day like getting the mail, taking out the trash, or reading a letter. For some reason, I just can't seem to connect my mind to my hands to write a simple thank-you note, boil noodles, or turn off the faucet after washing my hands. I do not like this new blurry-minded me. I just hope I am not in this state forever. I have been encouraged through counseling that this is a cycle of grief, but I am eagerly looking forward to this cycle being over.

I realize that a piece of me has been damaged. My heart is broken for the loss of my husband. Somehow, this brokenness has trickled into every part of my life, causing me to be a different person. I don't want to be a different person; I want to be the same old me.

When I first encountered you, my salvation affected everything about me. My heart was changed, my mind was transformed, and the way I saw the world and people around me completely shifted. I was wrecked; how did I ever live life without you?

I was not made for grief. This isn't the way you initially created the world to be. Through our sin, we violated the purity of creation which you intended. We gave up serene afternoons walking through beautiful gardens with you. We surrendered our communion with you. Grief is a violation on the creation you fashioned. Yet you made a way for our sin to be reconciled. Now when we experience loss, we have hope, because you made a way for us to be reunited with you after the pain of a loss. Though we still experience pain (the cost of sin we welcomed into creation), you surround us with the comfort of your hope.

It is still shocking to get used to grief, because we were not made for this kind of pain. Of course, I don't feel normal right now. This isn't how you initially created the world to be. But we hold something in our hearts that gets us through this suffering: hope.

Did Moses ever feel like an outsider, knowing he was an Israelite among Egyptians? I look to your Word and see that there must have been a season where Moses felt out of place.

> *One day, when Moses had grown up, he went out to his people and looked on their burdens, and he saw an Egyptian beating a Hebrew, one of his people. He looked this way and that, and seeing no one, he struck down the Egyptian and hid him in the sand.* (Exodus 2:11,12)

You were stirring something in his heart. You would use him to deliver the Israelites from the hands of Pharaoh. You would use Moses to deliver your people. The very thing that made him feel like an outsider, or simply just out of place, is the very thing you used for your glory and for the advancement of your kingdom.

> *By faith Moses, when he was born, was hidden for three months by his parents, because they saw that the child was beautiful, and they were not afraid of the king's edict. By faith Moses, when he was grown up, refused to be called the son of Pharaoh's daughter, choosing rather to be mistreated with the people of God than to enjoy the fleeting pleasures of sin.* (Hebrews 11:23–25)

Lord, use this season where I feel out of place and out of sorts to stir my heart in faith. Use my grief for your good.

> *By faith he left Egypt, not being afraid of the anger of the king, for he endured as seeing him who is invisible.* (Hebrews 11:27)

When I read about Moses, I see that your hand was always on his life. You planned every single second of his life, and you used every moment of his weakness for your glory. The things we deemed as small and trivial in Moses' life were pivotal moments you were orchestrating in your grand masterpiece. There is not a detail in the life of Moses that you did not use by your goodness and faithfulness.

I know that you will restore my life. I will look back on the moments I foolishly thought were overlooked and unseen by you and realize that you were using every discouraging piece of my story as a part of your plan for my life. I will look back on these days and see that your hand never stopped guiding my life.

If I Had Done Something Differently, Would Jordan Still Be Alive?

I replay moments with Jordan over and over in my head. If I had taken him to the hospital sooner, would he have lived? If I had made him eat healthier, or told him not to do certain activities, would he still be here with me? When we got married, did it make his life harder for him? I should have gone outside in the storm with him; then he wouldn't have fallen and broken his spine. I thought I did everything to keep him alive. I must have missed something. I was so shocked when he died.

I know that you were not surprised by the moment Jordan breathed his last breath. You knew the number of Jordan's days before you placed him in his mother's arms. His every breath here on earth, from the first to the last, are all recorded by you. I am comforted by this, but I still struggle with the weighty tension of resting in your sovereign hands while wrestling with my inner guilt. I remind myself that not one moment of my life is unseen by you. I also know that you do not make mistakes or happen upon accidents. Though I am wrestling inwardly, I know that what I did in the past does not thwart the ultimate plans of yours from happening. You are much too powerful for that nonsense. But what am I supposed to do with this knot of regret I feel deep in my gut? If only I had stayed with Jordan a little bit longer…

I know this isn't the first if-only you have ever heard. While I am feeling guilty about things I did and things I didn't do, I will do the only thing I know that I can do right now: rest in the palms of your sovereign hands. I know that at the end of the day, my plans do not prevail, but yours alone.

Many are the plans in the mind of a man, but it is the purpose of the Lord
that will stand. (Proverbs 19:21)

You are greater than my feelings. You are bigger than my broken heart. You have planned all of my days, the same as you had planned Jordan's days. When I look at all the things I should have done, instead of trusting that your will was done, I miss the fact that you are in control and you always have been.

In him we have obtained an inheritance, having been predestined according
to the purpose of him who works all things according to the counsel of his
will, so that we who were the first to hope in Christ might be to the praise
of his glory. (Ephesians 1:11,12)

I have to believe in your sovereignty. It is the only thing keeping me together in my downward spiral of what-ifs.

So, I will snuggle into the folds of your sovereign hands and let you minister to the aching depths of my soul. Your truth will give me freedom. My if-onlys and what-ifs are silenced by your warm and strong voice saying, "Only me."

"Remember not the former things, nor consider the things of old. Behold, I
am doing a new thing; now it springs forth, do you not perceive it? I will
make a way in the wilderness and rivers in the desert."
(Isaiah 43:18,19)

Did I Do Something Wrong to Deserve This?

After parking his walker, I took my regular position perched on the edge of the couch next to Jordan's chair. This was the closest seat next to my precious husband. Will I ever get to snuggle next to him like a regular newlywed couple?

I had to laugh at my own dream life—my dreams went from career promotions and oversea trips to wishing I could have a day with no hospital beeps or a night without breathing scares. I caught myself daydreaming about having a simple breakfast, sitting at a kitchen table, talking about the weather—nothing too serious. Is that too much to ask?

Now that Jordan is gone, my new life consists of waking up, a little bit of uncontrollable sobbing, doing a few house chores, a little more uncontrollable sobbing, checking the mail, and still more uncontrollable sobbing. I am tempted to think I must have done something wrong to deserve this pain.

I know this thought is absurd. I can think of the countless times I have done the unthinkable, yet you forgave me and gave me grace through my sinfulness. I can think of moments where I did not have faith, yet you still healed people miraculously. I can recall numerous mumblings of my heart, where I doubted your goodness, but that never stopped you from being good to me.

I can't help but think of Mary Magdalene, the woman you healed from seven demons. I wonder if she was known as "that demon-possessed lady." But you saw so much more in her.

Now when he rose early on the first day of the week, he appeared first to Mary Magdalene, from whom he had cast out seven demons. She went and told those who had been with him, as they mourned and wept. But when they heard that he was alive and had been seen by her, they would not believe it. (Mark 16:9–11)

Mary Magdalene was at your feet when you were crucified, and she was the first woman you appeared to when you rose from the grave. You did not see her through the lens of her past, but you loved her into her destiny.

Your grace for us sinners is more than generous. The very cross shows that I receive grace I do not deserve. You do not abuse me with suffering, you use my suffering for good!

Therefore, since we have been justified by faith, we have peace with God through our Lord Jesus Christ. Through him we have also obtained access by faith into this grace in which we stand, and we rejoice in hope of the glory of God. Not only that, but we rejoice in our sufferings, knowing that suffering produces endurance, and endurance produces character, and character produces hope, and hope does not put us to shame, because God's love has been poured into our hearts through the Holy Spirit who has been given to us. (Romans 5:1–5)

Out of the love you have poured into my heart, you use my suffering to produce endurance, character, and hope. You do not allow me to suffer in order for me to pay penance for my wrongdoings. You do not use our suffering as a payment, but you take our suffering and redeem it so that not one moment of our pain is wasted.

I Am Having Trouble Forgiving Myself

The hospital monitors' whistles and beeps had lulled to an occasional, muted hum. This was the hour when the unit became quieter than the usual hustle and bustle of poking and prodding, visitor check-ins and doctors' checkups. Now was the perfect time for Jordan to get some much-needed sleep. I slipped out of the room and asked my sweet mother-in-law to sit with him while I went to the restroom. On my way back, I decided to stop and get a cup of coffee. I filled my cup, taking a long, deep breath. I was getting my A-game ready for a long night. As I walked away from the coffee bar, I turned back, deciding I would splurge and get a flavored creamer for my coffee. Why not?

I made my way to our hospital room, walking slower than my usual pace. I was so surprised how quiet and peaceful the hospital could get in the middle of the night. I took it all in. As I approached our hospital room I could hear gasping. My heart dropped. I flung open the door to see my precious groom, grasping the sides of the bed and saying through suffocated pleas, "Where is Cady?"

I will never forget that moment. I neglected my own husband. Every minute I had with Jordan was precious and numbered. Any moment I was away from him was something precious I would never get back. But there I was, taking a casual stroll through the hospital hallways back to our room, while he was in the room afraid and in pain. I wasted priceless moments I could be at Jordan's side for what? Extra flavored coffee cream.

These kinds of memories are so difficult for me to reconcile. Now that he's gone, I kick myself for every second I wasted not being by his side, holding his hand, kissing his forehead—moments that were numbered and carelessly thrown away. I can't help but feel the weight of self-condemnation heavy on my shoulders.

I can relate with Paul when he says,

Wretched man that I am! Who will deliver me from this body of death? Thanks be to God through Jesus Christ our Lord! So then, I myself serve the law of God with my mind, but with my flesh I serve the law of sin.
(Romans 7:24,25)

But then he goes on to say,

There is therefore now no condemnation for those who are in Christ Jesus. For the law of the Spirit of life has set you free in Christ Jesus from the law of sin and death.
(Romans 8:1,2)

When my regrets turn into self-condemnation, I am turning away from the cross of Christ and walking into sin. When I take off the robes of righteousness that you wrapped around my broken body to put on the rags of filth and sin from which I am redeemed, I am ignoring what you did on the cross for me. You traded my rags for robes of righteousness when you gave your life for mine.

When I am riddled with regret, I will release my guilt into the hands that were nailed to a tree. When I am plagued with the lies of shame and remorse, I will proclaim the truth of the King who says I am his beloved. I will surrender my shame to you. And you will show me how to forgive myself.

The only way to reconcile these memories is to forgive myself and hold onto the sweet moments you gave me with Jordan. From what I have read about heaven, he is not dwelling on that moment I failed him. Where Jordan is now, he feels not a trace of pain. With this promise, I take great joy, knowing you have completely redeemed his broken body, and his spirit now lives with you. I need to rest in the reconciliation for myself. In every moment you have forgiven me, I need to boldly approach your throne of grace, knowing that it is your gift to me. Holding onto this burden will only keep me crippled with fear to love and live.

Let us then with confidence draw near to the throne of grace, that we may receive mercy and find grace to help in time of need.   (Hebrews 4:16)

The What-Ifs

There are so many things I wish Jordan were here to see. I imagine what life would be like if he could have seen his brothers getting married, his baby sisters growing into young women, and his nieces and nephews stepping into the world-changing individuals they already are.

I see him sharing inside jokes with his sisters-in-law, around mugs filled with steaming coffee, as the sound of rolling laughter fills the room. I see him snuggling his nieces and nephews, playing tag and airplane in a cozy living room cluttered with blocks and books. I see him reading stories to his sisters before bedtime, sneaking shared little giggles before he tucks them in for a good night's sleep.

These precious memories will never happen, and it crushes my heart to know it. There are so many little joys of Jordan's gentleness we will all miss out on, and some of his family members will never even experience. These thoughts are so difficult for me to reconcile. I don't understand why it has to be this way. I have to stop myself from thinking about it too much, otherwise I will go into a downward spiral of sadness.

> *And he led them out as far as Bethany, and lifting up his hands he blessed them. While he blessed them, he parted from them and was carried up into heaven. And they worshiped him and returned to Jerusalem with great joy, and were continually in the temple blessing God.* (Luke 24:50–53)

When you ascended into heaven, your people looked up to you with the twinkle of wonder in their eyes, but still had to blink away the tears to see their Messiah leave. I empathize with their confusion, wrestling with feelings of sadness while also trusting in the hope you promised them as a gift.

You didn't leave us alone while we wait. You sent us the Holy Spirit, the seal of our inheritance, to sustain our hearts until we are fully reunited with you.

"But you will receive power when the Holy Spirit has come upon you, and you will be my witnesses in Jerusalem and in all Judea and Samaria, and to the end of the earth." And when he had said these things, as they were looking on, he was lifted up, and a cloud took him out of their sight.

(Acts 1:8,9)

You didn't leave us. You didn't abandon us.

These dreams I have that I so desperately want may not happen on this side of heaven, but I know you have so much more waiting for me. When we are reunited with you, this sting of death I feel will have no trace on my soul. We will all gather at your table and laugh and feast together, in the presence of our Savior with no sorrow of missing out on what could have been. The fullness of your joy glorified in our bursting hearts, we will laugh and sing our praises to the one who never left us. The what-ifs I wrestled with not having here on earth will become fulfilled dreams in your kingdom.

Grocery Shopping for One

As I was perusing the aisles of my local grocery store, I couldn't help thinking of Jordan. It has taken me some time to get used to shopping for only one. There were certain treats he liked, and I frequently find myself walking down those aisles by habit, picking up the salt and vinegar chips for him, only to remember he won't be at home to enjoy them. I guess I don't need to sneak a pack of Sour Patch Kids into the cart today either. Yet I still throw them in my cart anyway; it's too difficult to pass up the memory.

In the dairy aisle, I start feeling my cheeks growing hot and my eyes starting to sting. *Oh no, not another cry fest in the middle of Walmart,* I think to myself.

I look down at my knuckles and see they are white from grasping the shopping cart handle so tightly. I can't help imagining Jordan's hand resting on mine.

But I know I am not alone. When the pangs of grief strike me at unexpected moments, you are the first to my side, comforting me, consoling me, and simply being near to me. Not a moment of heartache is too small for you.

When these moments of grief interrupt my normal day-to-day chores, you rush to my aid and let me know that I am not alone. You walk with me, up and down the aisles, your warm hand on mine as I secretly cry a little while sifting through the produce. The moment I think I am utterly alone, you always show up. Whether it's looking through old photos of Jordan or doing something as simple as walking beside me through the bread aisle, you are near me.

"Fear not, for I am with you; be not dismayed, for I am your God; I will strengthen you, I will help you, I will uphold you with my righteous right hand."
(Isaiah 41:10)

I couldn't have gotten through this grocery run without you.

I Just Tried to Text Jordan

There is a first for everything.

I'm a late bloomer in this, but today was the first time I tried to text Jordan. Wow. Such a surreal experience. It's been over a year since he has been in heaven with you. Did I forget for a second that he is not here anymore, but with you? After realizing that I was texting Jordan (as if he had never been gone), it made me think about how eternal you are.

If there is one thing I have learned in this past year, it would be this: your comfort is very real and very near. You have shown me so much throughout these past months of grieving. I have learned that you will never leave me stuck in a place of hopelessness. I have also learned that I am never helpless. On my own I am helpless, but with you I am an overcomer. And the best part of this truth is that I am never without you. Even when I have doubts whether you are near me, you are standing right in front of me, leveling mountains and calling my name through the darkness. I can look back and see that you had me in your hands every single second.

You hem me in, behind and before, and lay your hand upon me. Such knowledge is too wonderful for me; it is high; I cannot attain it.

(Psalm 139:5,6)

I am in awe of how you can submerge yourself into the middle of my raging seas and speak peace over my heart while simultaneously calling me forward into your light. I can try my best to run away from you, but there is nowhere I can hide from your love. You go before me and you stand behind me. There is not a single second I am without you. I am comforted knowing that I am completely surrounded by you.

I Found a Box
of Jordan's Clothes

I wasn't expecting to find a box of Jordan's clothes while cleaning out my closet today. I finally decided to tackle this chore and was not looking forward to it. I think deep down I knew there would be a few boxes I didn't feel ready to open. When I came across the box of his clothes, my eyes instantly filled with tears. I immediately started smelling every piece of clothing, taking in the scent of his aftershave. I remember ironing these shirts for him before he went to work. I remember how the shoulder of his suit jacket felt against my face when I would hug him goodbye in the morning. I grabbed my favorite shirt of his from the box and held it close to my heart. My heart was flooded with the same feelings I had when he proposed to me in this shirt.

I think of Joseph of Arimathea, and how he wrapped your body in linens and placed you in a tomb after you had been crucified. He must have felt hopeless, wrapping the body of the Messiah, once perfect and without blemish, now marred with marks of a torturous death.

And Joseph bought a linen shroud, and taking him down, wrapped him in the linen shroud and laid him in a tomb that had been cut out of the rock. And he rolled a stone against the entrance of the tomb. (Mark 15:46)

Little did your followers know that in three days, they would find that linen folded and the tomb empty, for you had finished what you came to earth to do—reconcile us back to you. Your life didn't end in that tomb; the tombstone rolled away, showing us that this is the beginning of new life with you.

But the angel said to the women, "Do not be afraid, for I know that you seek Jesus who was crucified. He is not here, for he has risen, as he said. Come, see the place where he lay. Then go quickly and tell his disciples that he has risen from the dead, and behold, he is going before you to Galilee; there you will see him. See, I have told you."   (Matthew 28:5–7)

Though my closet is full of Jordan's clothes, my comfort is found in the empty tomb, where the only thing remaining was the folded linen that once wrapped your body.

Today Is Jordan's Birthday

Happy birthday, Jordan Alexander. You changed my life. You lived every second to love others. Today I will celebrate your precious life. And cry. While eating cake.

Why are birthdays so hard? It feels like I am starting all over again in the grief process. I have this weight deep in my heart that feels insurmountable. I try to breathe in more deeply to release the pain, but it still sits there heavily on my chest, like a stone at the bottom of the sea.

It is hard not to imagine what it would be like to have Jordan here for his birthday. I will never see him develop deep crinkles around his eyes or get gray hair. What would he have dreamed of doing next? What would have been his next goal to conquer? Would we have had any fun trips planned together?

I am so sad that I am not throwing Jordan a birthday party today. He was always so fun to celebrate. He never wanted the attention, but totally deserved a parade (in my humble opinion). It is crazy to think that today is another birthday being celebrated in heaven instead of here on earth. Which place would host the best birthday party? That's a no-brainer. I'm pretty sure Jesus has this day covered with party festivities. (I'm sure Moses and C. S. Lewis are in charge of the party hats!)

Let's be honest, Jordan does not even care that it's his birthday today. He is having too much fun on heavenly adventures with you. He is so wrapped up in your glory, praising your wonderful name, that he doesn't feel a trace of sadness or emptiness. The only ones who really need cake on Jordan's birthday are all of us loved ones left here on earth.

I know that the same divine joy that floods through heaven's gates will flood into my heart and comfort me. You know the moments of today that will be difficult for me. I will start this day in your Word, pouring out my praise and sorrow to you. You comfort me with your Scriptures, showing me that today is a day that you are near my heart.

When the L<small>ORD</small> *restored the fortunes of Zion, we were like those who dream. Then our mouth was filled with laughter, and our tongue with shouts of joy; then they said among the nations, 'The* L<small>ORD</small> *has done great things for them.' The* L<small>ORD</small> *has done great things for us; we are glad.*

Restore our fortunes, O L<small>ORD</small>, *like streams in the Negeb! Those who sow in tears shall reap with shouts of joy! He who goes out weeping, bearing the seed for sowing, shall come home with shouts of joy, bringing his sheaves with him.* (Psalm 126:1–6)

I Am in Despair

I am in total despair. I feel as if I am alone and you have abandoned me. When I look to the right or to the left, I see nothing but ruins. My life is in shambles. When I think of my past with Jordan, it is riddled with regret. When I think of my future without him, I feel overwhelmed. I am crying out to you for help, for that is the only thing I know I can do.

> O LORD, how long shall I cry for help, and you will not hear? Or cry to you "Violence!" and you will not save? Why do you make me see iniquity, and why do you idly look at wrong? Destruction and violence are before me; strife and contention arise. (Habakkuk 1:2,3)

In these verses, I imagine Habakkuk shaking his fists at the heavens with tears streaming down his face. The utter despair of Habakkuk comforts my heart. You are a perfect God, yet you wove the cries of Habakkuk questioning your character into your Scripture. His cry is desperate, and his plea is accusatory of your good will. Yet you answer him with hope.

> "Look among the nations, and see; wonder and be astounded. For I am doing a work in your days that you would not believe if told." (Habakkuk 1:5)

You encourage Habakkuk to look to you and see that you will do a mighty redemptive work to restore the people of Judah. But he still doesn't believe you are going to rescue them from the destructive turmoil of the Babylonians. So, he responds:

> I will take my stand at my watchpost and station myself on the tower, and look out to see what he will say to me, and what I will answer concerning my complaint. (Habakkuk 2:1)

How many times have I spoken to you like this? You promise that your hand is at work, yet I challenge you with a smart-alec tone, challenging your faithfulness. But you, in all your grace and goodness, respond to me like you did to Habakkuk:

> *And the LORD answered me: "Write the vision; make it plain on tablets, so he may run who reads it. For still the vision awaits its appointed time; it hastens to the end—it will not lie. If it seems slow, wait for it; it will surely come; it will not delay."* (Habakkuk 2:2,3)

You continue to encourage Habakkuk to hold on to the vision you have given him. You reassure him that your timing is perfect and that you have a plan. And, of course, we see in these three short chapters of Habakkuk that you restore his faith and breathe hope into his despair. His tone is completely different from just two chapters earlier when he was filing his complaints with the Maker of the universe.

> *Yet I will rejoice in the LORD; I will take joy in the God of my salvation. GOD, the Lord, is my strength; he makes my feet like the deer's; he makes me tread on my high places.* (Habakkuk 3:18,19)

Lord, change my song like you changed the song of Habakkuk. Pull me out of my despair and remind me of the vision you have for my life. You are my strength when I am weak and accusatory. You sustain me while I wait for you. I will rejoice in you, for you alone are my salvation.

I Have a Sinking Feeling in My Gut That Won't Go Away

It's 3 a.m. and I am wide awake. The pillow does not have a cool side after I've repeatedly flipped it over, the covers have been fluffed to the fluffiest degree, I have now finished two cups of chamomile tea, and I have even tried counting sheep—which is a total joke, in my humble opinion.

My mind is spinning about my future. My heart is heavy with worry. I am concerned about bills, and I am afraid about debt. I am also trying to figure out how you will somehow restore my dreams of having children. I feel like I take each day moment by moment, holding my breath while praying to you.

I wonder if this is what the Israelites felt as Micah prophesied the coming of the Messiah. I am sure their hearts were longing for salvation. Vulnerable to enemy attack without a king, they were desperately awaiting the coming of the Messiah, the one who would deliver them from the hands of their enemies. This prophecy foretells of a hope that would change the course of history. You would not only restore the lineage of your people, but you would heal the entire world from utter brokenness.

I can relate with the heaviness the Israelites must have felt while waiting for you. Were they taking each day moment by moment because it was all they could do to keep breathing? Were they emotionally heavy with worry? Were they too afraid to dream of restoration of their lands?

Nestled in the middle of this life-changing, history-shifting prophecy, Micah proclaims:

> And he shall stand and shepherd his flock in the strength of the LORD, in the majesty of the name of the LORD his God. And they shall dwell secure, for now he shall be great to the ends of the earth. And he shall be their peace. (Micah 5:4,5)

You prophesied through Micah to restore the hope of your broken and directionless children. You proclaimed hope over every dreamless future and every broken dream. The Messiah would come, and he would restore his people.

I will stand secure in you and you will shepherd me—through this sleepless night, through my stacks of bills, through my endless questions of, "What now?"

When you stepped down from your throne and into the heart of a flawed woman, you, in full deity, knew I would be lying awake tonight afraid, overwhelmed, and directionless.

But this isn't where you will leave me.

Just as you restored the hopes of your people that miraculous night in Bethlehem, which would lead to the cross at Calvary, bringing your children back to your heart, you will restore the turmoil that has shattered my life. You have breathed your promises of hope into my broken dreams. You will be my peace.

Going to a Party Alone

I really don't want to go to this party alone. The social awkwardness of it all is almost unbearable. I know everyone is wondering how they should even approach conversation with me. I'm sure they are thinking the same question I would be thinking: "Should I ask her about Jordan or not?"

Lord, you hold every astronomical sphere in your hand, breathing it into orbit, and somehow my world just seems far too big for me. Light-years and galaxies, vast regions and ocean depths, are just pieces of your creation I will never be able to fully explore in my lifetime. Yet you step down into this small moment of a dinner party to remind me that I am not alone and that you are always right beside me.

As I get ready for this party and mentally prepare myself to walk in without my arm hooked in Jordan's, I will stand strong knowing that I am going into this dinner party with someone who walked this moment before me. I will remember whose I am. Thank you for seeing me in every crowded room.

"It is the Lord who goes before you. He will be with you; he will not leave you or forsake you. Do not fear or be dismayed." (Deuteronomy 31:8)

Socially Awkward

"So, you got any kids? How long have you been married?"

Oh dear, I think to myself, *you don't want to know.*

The maintenance man stands there silent, wrench in hand. Leaky faucet. Something Jordan would've tried to fix. He may not have known how, but he still would've tried. I loved that about him. I look down at my wedding ring sparkling on my hand.

"I'm actually widowed. Cancer." I exhale quickly as I try to get my bullet-point response out in one breath. It seems to make it easier, or at least that's what I tell myself. My strategy is to tell people up front; the sooner I get it over with, the sooner I don't have to worry about my weird story anymore.

Poor guy. All he came to do was fix my faucet, not to hear a sob story. He wasn't expecting additional water works from a widowed wife.

This social encounter is my new typical routine. I either tell everyone too much about Jordan, or I don't tell them enough until I drop the widow-bomb on them and they start to feel bad for something they said to me earlier in conversation.

I have also noticed that I love talking about Jordan. I try to make sure I bring him up as much as possible to ensure that he won't be forgotten. After all, it is up to me to carry his memory, or so I've told myself.

One time, when a friend told a hysterical joke at lunch with a group of other friends, it struck my funny bone apparently because I started laughing hysterically. I then realized I was laughing for the first time in months. The realization struck me so poignantly that I started bawling while simultaneously laughing at the joke. Yea, it was weird. You can imagine the faces of the people gathered around. I rushed off to the bathroom as quickly as possible.

I have to admit I am embarrassed at how awkward I can get in a social gathering, but I know I need to see my socially awkward state as a battle wound from losing my spouse, not as a personality deficiency I need to feel insecure about. I know this will not last forever, and I need to give myself a little more grace.

> *For everything there is a season, and a time for every matter under heaven: a time to be born, and a time to die; a time to plant, and a time to pluck up what is planted; a time to kill, and a time to heal; a time to break down, and a time to build up; a time to weep, and a time to laugh; a time to mourn, and a time to dance.* (Ecclesiastes 3:1–4)

Even as I am writing down these recent awkward moments I have had in public, I can't help but let out a chuckle. This is another season that will soon pass. Until then, I will rest in knowing that you are working in me. Grief can encompass everything in my mind, but you hold me closer and encourage me when I feel like I am overwhelmed. My mourning will soon be a time of dancing.

Why Am I So Absent-Minded?

I went to run some errands for the church today. I knew I needed to make a quick stop at the nearest craft store for some project supplies; we are starting a new series at church and I was looking forward to getting some decorations for the church lobby. This craft store is a routine stop for me, and I have grown up going to this store.

I must have been thinking about something else, but I could not seem to find this craft store no matter how hard I tried! I got turned around three times thinking I was going in the right direction. When I made my fourth U-turn in the middle of a four-lane street, I saw the police lights in my rearview mirror. My heart sank. I know I look like a loony driver! I pull over as quickly as I can, as I can feel my heart beat faster. I am starting to rehearse what I will say to the police officer, but to be honest, I am drawing a blank. I really do not know why I have no idea which way I need to turn to get to the craft store, or why I am driving like an idiot. I also feel a little caught off guard because I'm still trying to figure out how I just got lost in my own hometown.

I start to pull out my driver's license and registration and I see a familiar face dressed in uniform in the side mirror.

"Cady? Is that you?" I roll down my window.

At this point I have tears stinging in my eyes and I really don't know why.

"Are you okay? Do you need any help?"

The policeman who pulled me over just so happens to be a part of our church's security team. I have to admit, I don't even mind if I get a ticket at this point—in fact I knew I deserved one with my crazy driving—I just need somebody to help me and I need a second to catch my breath. Seeing a familiar face to help me out of my frantic state brought so much relief to my heart, I could instantly feel the tears burning behind my eyes.

The police officer's voice was calm and gentle. "It's okay, Cady. Just take a second and breathe. Do you need me to help you get to your next stop?"

I shook my head. "I'm sorry, I'm driving like a crazy person. I think I'm just going to sit here a second and catch my breath."

He nodded. "Okay, well you let me know if there's anything I can do. Take your time, okay?"

I don't know why, but I get lost a lot now. I forget names, I lose things, I can stare at a menu for thirty minutes and not even know what it says. I can't tell you how many times I've walked into a grocery store and walked out forty-five minutes later with nothing. What am I doing in grocery stores for that long? And what did I come here to get again?

I sort of feel like it's a type of mental response to my grief. My mind is constantly functioning at the highest capacity, trying to make sense of this new life without Jordan. All gaskets are operating at full speed attempting to process my heartache. There is no remaining room for simple things like remembering the way to the craft store just down the street, or knowing how to drive like a normal person.

The forgetfulness is so sneaky too. I don't really know I'm operating in absent-mindedness until a moment brings me back to reality and I realize that my heat is aching, and my mind is operating at 110 percent to try to make the pain stop.

I'm so touched by this moment with the police officer because it reminded me of how much grace God has for me in this time of weakness. He even used an officer in that moment of absentmindedness to get me pulled over, give me a second to breath, and get my head on straight! Otherwise, I probably could've gotten into a wreck!

When my mind is racing, or when I've called the locksmith (he's now saved in my phone) for the fourth time because I locked my keys in the car again, I just have to laugh at myself, and know that this isn't my forever.

"Therefore I tell you, do not be anxious about your life, what you will eat or what you will drink, nor about your body, what you will put on. Is not life

more than food, and the body more than clothing? Look at the birds of the air: they neither sow nor reap nor gather into barns, and yet your heavenly Father feeds them. Are you not of more value than they? And which of you by being anxious can add a single hour to his span of life?"

(Matthew 6:25–27)

Time and time again you cease my anxious thoughts with your love. You hold birds in your hands and clothe them, so they are warm in the winter. You hold me close to your heart and quiet my mind with your promises of truth. And sometimes, you show your comforting presence in very tangible ways, like a gracious officer not giving me a speeding ticket.

Some of My Friends Have Stepped Away

I was warned about this. I knew it could happen but didn't actually think it would happen to me. My friend has completely gone "MIA" on me. As soon as Jordan died, it was as if she couldn't handle the grief—that the pain was too much for her to deal with—so she completely disappeared. She hasn't checked in on me, and she hasn't answered my texts. I'm trying so hard not to be offended, but honestly, her absence in my life has really broken my heart. Now is the time I need her in my life the most. Of all times to choose to be absent in my life, why now? I've just lost my husband and I could really use a friend right now just to talk to.

A man of many companions may come to ruin, but there is a friend who sticks closer than a brother. (Proverbs 18:24)

Lord, you are closer than kin, closer than blood. You know everything about me, before I even know what I'm feeling or why I am feeling it. When I lash out, you hold me. When I despair, you remind me that I belong to you. When I question your goodness, you whisper your promises over me. When I weep, you weep with me. No friend on this earth can ever compare to the faithful friend you have been for me.

The death of Jordan wasn't hard only for me. It was hard for my friend too. It's not natural to go through death; no one knows exactly the right thing to say or do when it happens. She doesn't know how to process this season of my life and I shouldn't expect her to even know how to handle these emotions I am experiencing, but I am still hurt by her abandonment. Therefore, I will do what you've always told me to do when another person has offended me: I will pray for my friend.

Lord, would you be near my friend who is confused and hurting? Would you be as close to her broken heart as you have been to mine?

Walk her through how to reconcile the broken pieces grief leaves behind and knit her heart back together. Silence any self-condemnation, confusion, or despair she may be battling. Would you comfort her with your sweet presence and minister to her with your words of love? Let her feel your peace surrounding her. In Jesus' name, amen.

Even writing this prayer for her has caused me to feel your grace for her. I know she is hurting too, and that you will be near to her just as you have been so close to me.

You are closer than a brother, carrying me through the turmoil and ruin that is all around me. I may see buildings crumble and cities fall on both sides of me, but your strong arms will carry me through this grieving season of brokenness.

Though I may have friends who fall out of my life, that is okay. There is an abundant grace for them just as you have shown your grace to me by bringing me new friends—and even strangers—to take my hands and walk through this with me. I have not been abandoned, but lavishly surrounded.

Am I Going Crazy?

Today I had to laugh when I looked at myself in the mirror. At some point in the day I managed to put my sweater on inside out and backwards. Seriously? Both inside out *and* backwards?! I knew this sweater didn't feel like it fit me right. Oh well, at least my hair is brushed. One time I kept a curler in my hair for the entire day until, to my utter dismay, I scratched my head while talking to someone in the grocery store and felt it still lodged in the back of my head! Oh, and the timing was perfect, because the girl I ran into had just asked me how I was doing, to which I replied, "I'm actually doing pretty good!" Great. Now she will be able to call my bluff.

I know I am really not okay, but I am desperately trying to convince everyone else that I am doing just fine. I am even trying to convince myself. Why am I trying to convince myself that I am okay when I know I am not? I know me, I know the truth. Why am I lying to myself?

But Zion said, "The LORD has forsaken me; my Lord has forgotten me."

"Can a woman forget her nursing child, that she should have no compassion on the son of her womb? Even these may forget, yet I will not forget you."
(Isaiah 49:14,15)

You know I am one step away from completely losing my mind. You know how I am balancing on a tight rope of mental sanity; wobbling, shaking, I am just hoping I won't fall off into the unknown abyss. I feel as though I am one slip away from what society calls "crazy."

You see right through me.

You know I had a bag of chips for breakfast, and I forgot to turn off the water after I showered. You know that my new apartment is still cluttered with unpacked boxes and unwashed dishes. You know that I have a ridiculous amount of unread texts and emails. The thought of attempting to address either of these tasks is not only overwhelming but crippling to me.

You may be the only one who knows how many times I have left the milk out on the counter to spoil, and how many times I locked my keys in the car. (Last time it was running for two hours before I realized what I had done!) But I also know that it is normal to feel like I am going crazy during this time of grief. I am comforted in knowing that I may forget things, but I am not overlooked by you. I may forget a curler in my hair, but you will never forget me.

I Wish I Could Have Just One More Conversation with Jordan

If I was stuck in traffic on the way home from work, I'd always call Jordan. If I wanted a safe place to speak my mind or talk through a hard day, I had Jordan. I just got home from running errands and I am sipping tea alone at the dining room table. I turned on all the lamps and the television to make it feel less empty in here, but the truth is, my heart would not feel any less lonely if I were sitting in a crowded room.

It's not even the big things I want to talk about with Jordan, just little things that only he would understand—like how proud I am that my one and only houseplant is still alive, that the grocery store finally started carrying our favorite cold brew coffee, and how I saw my first monarch butterfly of the year. He would also be very proud to know that I finally organized the junk drawer we were always joking about. I never realized what a treasure it was to have someone who knew and loved my soul to share small talk with at the end of the day.

Sure, I have big questions I would love to ask Jordan about. But it's the little side conversations I miss more frequently. There are some days I feel this wish burning deep inside my chest: if I could have just one more conversation with him, I would . . . What would I say? I would love the dialogue, but I would know that eventually the conversation would have to come to an end.

Lord, I am going to talk to you. I know you always hear me. I may be the only one sitting at the dining room table right now, but I know that you are near me. Today I will share with you the small things that made me smile because one thing I know about you is that although you are all-knowing and all-powerful, you still want to hear about my day.

Surely goodness and mercy shall follow me all the days of my life, and I shall dwell in the house of the LORD forever. (Psalm 23:6)

"I will not leave you as orphans; I will come to you." (John 14:18)

I Need to Hear Your Voice

When I look back at my journey and see that I am still standing, I can't help seeing that your hand was guiding my every step and holding me up when I was too weak to stand. Some steps were rocky, and I stumbled along the path, but some steps were strong and steadfast.

Although I can see the works of your hands in my life, I feel like I haven't heard your voice in a while. I desperately want to. It is like I can see your hand orchestrating every note and every measure of my song. Not one note is unseen by your beautiful hands, as you sketch the ballad of my journey. When will I hear the melody you are singing over me? Am I too deeply entangled in the clamor of my own grief that I cannot hear the song you are proclaiming over me?

The word of the LORD came to Jeremiah a second time, while he was still shut up in the court of the guard. (Jeremiah 33:1)

In Jeremiah's moments of imprisonment for prophesying the Babylonian siege on Jerusalem, you still spoke to him. Nothing will stop you from speaking to us. While he was in prison, you continued to speak to him, sharing your promises and your hope for the future of your people. You bring us hope even in the dark cells of a prison.

"Call to me and I will answer you, and will tell you great and hidden things that you have not known." (Jeremiah 33:3)

When I am in the gallows of sorrow, you speak to me no matter where I am, freeing my soul from sadness. Like Jeremiah shut up in the court of the guard, no place is beyond the range of your voice. And you continue to speak to my heart through Scripture even though sometimes I feel like I'm not hearing anything.

And this city shall be to me a name of joy, a praise and a glory before all the nations of the earth who shall hear of all the good that I do for them. They shall fear and tremble because of all the good and all the prosperity I provide for it. (Jeremiah 33:9)

Even in our imprisonment, you speak your promises to us. You remind us of your extravagant plans and what you are doing.

"Therefore, behold, I will allure her, and bring her into the wilderness, and speak tenderly to her. And there I will give her her vineyards and make the Valley of Achor a door of hope. And there she shall answer as in the days of her youth, as at the time when she came out of the land of Egypt." (Hosea 2:14,15)

How Will This Ever Be Good?

Life is full of tastes and sips of what is to come when we are finally reunited with you. Each little glimmer of your kingdom is sent from you to keep us hopeful while we wait until we are with you. You hold us over with a foretaste of grace so we can keep running the race. I have learned through this process of grief that we will never be fully satisfied until we are reunited with you.

I think about heaven more than I ever have before. I think about the cross and what you did for me from a whole new perspective. The cross resonates with my soul in a way it never did before Jordan died. Because of the cross, I have heaven to look forward to and give me hope. You used this whole experience of suffering in so many ways, but I treasure what you have done for me on a whole new level of appreciation for my salvation in you.

There are still so many mysteries about my suffering that I have yet to understand, but I also know that you are doing things in me that I have yet to discover. Until then, I wait.

> *For with the LORD there is steadfast love, and with him is plentiful redemption.* (Psalm 130:7)

I know how you work, Lord. I have seen it for myself. Though I am downtrodden and discouraged, you remind me that you will not leave me here in this season of sadness. Just as the winter melts into spring, so will this hopelessness melt into beautiful blossoms of joy. I may not know what you are doing in my life right now, or how you will bring goodness out of this situation, but I trust that your hand is at work. So far you have proven yourself as unfailing. You are in the business of making horrible things somehow turn out good. Until then, I will wait. You will turn my ashes of mourning into something beautiful.

> *...to grant to those who mourn in Zion—to give them a beautiful headdress instead of ashes, the oil of gladness instead of mourning, the garment of praise instead of a faint spirit; that they may be called oaks of righteousness, the planting of the Lord, that he may be glorified.* (Isaiah 61:3)

Our Song

As I was driving home, I turned on the radio. There it was. Our song. Playing as if no one had a care in the world, or no time had passed, or no one listening to the radio had an emotional attachment to its melody. Our song played on the radio unapologetically, filling my car with uninvited memories and unwelcome tears. I was instantly taken to a time of impromptu slow dancing, really bad lip-syncing, and hand holding. I am fortunate that I heard our song for the first time in my car while driving alone instead of in some random public place—or a wedding! Could you even imagine?

Lord, hearing our song today was hard enough. Will this song always bring back so many memories?

It feels like it's easier to think Jordan is here than to remember he is gone. There are so many little moments throughout the day when I feel like he is still here. I miss those moments of us looking at each other, knowing exactly what the other person was thinking. Then there are those times when a TV commercial comes on that we always thought was funny, or I find something that makes me want to tap his shoulder to talk about it. I never knew how many little special moments we shared on a daily basis until he went to heaven.

Alas, these are moments that are only mine to cherish. I can look back at these recollections as the painful past, or I can look at them as precious gifts from you. Every memory with Jordan is a sweet gift you gave exclusively to me. I have many of them, which shows how generously you poured out your love to me.

Our song is now finishing up on the radio, but in my heart, I can hear another song playing. It is the song you are singing over me. You are near my heart singing over my sorrow, reminding me that I can look into my future with hope. There are more precious memories to come.

The Lord bless you and keep you; the Lord make his face to shine upon you and be gracious to you; the Lord lift up his countenance upon you and give you peace. (Numbers 6:24–26)

I Just Paid Off a Loan by Myself

I did something today: I paid off my car. Jordan would have been so proud of me. I am so proud I independently did something that was financially wise. Granted, I did it with the money he left me, but still, I am not only surviving the wreckage of grief, I'm paying off debts!

It was strange when I went to the bank to pay off my remaining balance. Although I'm deeply joyful and proud of myself, I couldn't help feeling a sting of pain in my gut. Paying off the loan today was something I wanted to do with Jordan. Paying off this loan also shows that I am in a new place of independence, dealing with things I used to not have to think about on my own. Paying off this loan shows me that life is still moving forward, whether Jordan is here or not. This made me feel sad, because Jordan was irreplaceable. Sometimes I wish the world would just stop to acknowledge he isn't here anymore.

I always thought that if I lost him I would be a complete wreck. Emotionally, I have been. But to look at myself making a significant financial decision without consulting my partner in life is sort of sobering. I am seeing that I am capable of living without him. And this makes me feel empty inside, like I am moving forward with the rest of the world too.

These strange feelings of independence and grief are like a two-way street. In one lane, I'm amazed at how you have healed and matured my heart, showing me that I can withstand more than I ever thought I could. In the other lane, I feel like I'm driving alone, and at every turn I am reminded that I don't have my teammate in the car with me, helping me navigate the curves of the winding road.

But there's another piece to this visual analogy that I am forgetting to mention. I forgot to mention who is driving the car and who has been guiding and directing this ride since the very beginning. You are the one with the hands on the wheel gently steering me away from potholes and navigating me away from ditches, completely controlling this journey. Although it may be filled with rocky roads, narrow paths up steep mountains, or endless roads through miles of desert, you are always in control, guiding my heart through every single obstacle.

I realize today marks a day that I never thought I would do alone. We will get through this together. When I can't see what lies before me, you can. Your calming presence guides me through the ups and downs of life, showing me that I am not alone.

I paid off my car loan all by myself today, and you helped me do it.

The LORD appeared to him from far away. I have loved you with an everlasting love; therefore I have continued my faithfulness to you.

(Jeremiah 31:3)

Revisiting Places with Bad Memories

I used to live my life in a hospital room. Bandages and blood, wires and IVs, surgical equipment and hospital beeps were a regular day-to-day experience for me. We were in Oklahoma City for a very risky brain surgery to help remove the aggressive tumor that was taking Jordan's life. My time sleeping in a chair beside him in the ICU was the most frightening experience I had ever walked through at that point in time.

The medical professionals told us a lot of things could go wrong. I stayed up all night watching him, crying, and begging you to deliver us from this pain. I would read Psalm 91 over and over into the wee hours of the night. Those Scriptures were my only source of sanity.

Needless to say, I was not a fan of Oklahoma City. Too many horrific memories, and that city knew all of them.

Because he holds fast to me in love, I will deliver him; I will protect him, because he knows my name. (Psalm 91:14)

Now I live in Oklahoma City. I have been all around the areas I vowed never to return to. I have had the sweetest memories—redemptive memories—of belly laughter, family outings, and birthday parties in the same parking lots I used to cry in. I happily live here and adore every moment I'm here—something I never thought would be possible. The very ruins I treaded upon are now my trails of joy.

"When he calls to me, I will answer him; I will be with him in trouble; I will rescue him and honor him. With long life I will satisfy him and show him my salvation." (Psalm 91:15,16)

Little did I know that the sleepless nights I proclaimed Psalm 91 over Jordan's life were actually going to come to pass in my life as your redemptive promises of restoration for me. I didn't want it that way, but now I can't imagine having my story written in any other way.

I was the one who needed rescuing.

First Christmas without Jordan

This is my first Christmas without Jordan. The heartache I feel is unbearable. Nothing looks the same, and nothing feels the same. This holiday used to be the most awaited time of the year for me. Now, it is tainted with a type of sadness I can't even put into words. Like the blankets of snow outside of my window, my sadness covers all that was vibrant in a sheet of sorrow. I am trying my hardest to be cheerful and to be "normal." I go through the motions and the traditions, but it's just not the same without Jordan here.

It helps if I keep busy, but if I try to recreate what Jordan and I did in the past for our Christmas traditions, it hurts even more. It reminds me of what I'm missing and why this Christmas, and all other Christmases, will never be the same.

> *And in the same region there were shepherds out in the field, keeping watch over their flock by night. And an angel of the Lord appeared to them, and the glory of the Lord shone around them, and they were filled with great fear. And the angel said to them, "Fear not, for behold, I bring you good news of great joy that will be for all the people. For unto you is born this day in the city of David a Savior, who is Christ the Lord."*
>
> (Luke 2:8–11)

When the world was waiting for your arrival, I imagine a similar gloom blanketed the earth in a dew of hopelessness because the Messiah had not yet come. But you sustained the hearts of your people with prophecies and signs, stirring up the anticipation that you would return to save your dying world.

In my season of sorrow, I still have the deepest of joys. I am reminded of the shepherds keeping watch over their flocks by night. They had no idea what they were missing until the host of angels appeared in the night sky, flooding the heavens with light and flooding their hearts with hope.

Long-awaiting for you to return, the universe had no idea what was in store for our rescue. You came to the earth fully human and fully king, your majesty dwelling in a temple of human flesh and bones, bearing a message of hope: you have come to save your people.

I will shed a lot of tears this Christmas. Last night, we did our family tradition of seeing a movie at the theatre after we had our Christmas dinner. I left in the middle of the movie and hid in a bathroom stall, crying for a good forty-five minutes.

My mom knocked on my door right after I excused myself to go to bed for the night. "Can I come sleep with you? I don't want you to sleep alone tonight." We fell asleep, with hurting hearts but holding hands.

"As one whom his mother comforts, so I will comfort you; you shall be comforted in Jerusalem." (Isaiah 66:13)

You see me, Lord. You sent my mother to come in my room at the right moment, even when I didn't know that I was needing a special moment of comfort.

I know one thing about your comforting grace: while you are big enough to redeem a fallen world, you are still gentle enough to comfort my broken heart on Christmas Eve. I will trust you to hold me through every moment this holiday season. You will soothe my heartache and remind me that when you changed the course of history by sending your Son, you painted a new story for all of us. Because of your sacrifice, I know I will see Jordan again. But mostly, I will be reunited with you. You are the rescuer indeed.

I cry aloud to God, aloud to God, and he will hear me. (Psalm 77:1)

I'm Feeling Hopeless

Hope is such a silly thing. Hope stands in front of me, arms wide open, ready to fully embrace me with promises of a better tomorrow. But sometimes I am too afraid to take the hand of hope, because it could be a scary journey that requires me to leave my safe little corner. What if I go on this adventure with hope and am left more empty than I am feeling now?

Sometimes I have my hands over my ears blocking out your sweet voice of hope whispering promises of joy and a future over me. In these moments, I find that I am too afraid to have hope, because what if my situation is beyond repair?

There is one thing I have that cannot be taken from me: your everlasting, heart-pursuing, standard-shifting love. Your love stands in the shadows of my dark bedroom, reminding me there is so much more in store for me in this life. You show me your love through an acquaintance who left a frozen dinner on my front porch in case I get hungry and don't have the energy to cook. When I feel forgotten or unseen, you show me your love through the mystery person who paid for my lunch today. You show me your love through extravagant sacrifice and small acts of kindness throughout the day. Through your love, you give me hope. You pursue me with your love and lift my eyes to see the hope you have for me.

Hope is knowing that life with you is the ultimate treasure, and I will see your face soon. Because of your love for me, you changed the course of history by sending your Son as my ransom though I deserved the death sentence for my sin. This is my ultimate hope, knowing that I will be reunited with my King and all the saints whom he saved through his sacrifice. Today I am sad, but I have the sweetest gift deep down inside my soul—your hope.

"I will bless her, and moreover, I will give you a son by her. I will bless her, and she shall become nations; kings of peoples shall come from her." Then

Abraham fell on his face and laughed and said to himself, "Shall a child be born to a man who is a hundred years old? Shall Sarah, who is ninety years old, bear a child?" (Genesis 17:16,17)

So Sarah laughed to herself, saying, "After I am worn out, and my lord is old, shall I have pleasure?" The LORD said to Abraham, "Why did Sarah laugh and say, 'Shall I indeed bear a child, now that I am old?' Is anything too hard for the Lord? At the appointed time I will return to you, about this time next year, and Sarah shall have a son." (Genesis 18:12,13)

Did Sarah feel afraid to hope when you promised her a son at her old age? Did she laugh out of self-defense, to cover up that flicker of hope that you could indeed give her a child?

But you graciously credit her as righteousness for her faith even though she laughed in disbelief.

By faith Sarah herself received power to conceive, even when she was past the age, since she considered him faithful who had promised. (Hebrews 11:11)

I can only imagine the bouts of hopelessness she struggled with while holding onto your promise that she would have a son. My heart feels not so alone knowing that even in your Scriptures, there are women who experienced this similar tension of walking on the tightrope of hope. Having faith can be scary, because we put our hope on the line. When we have faith, we put our assurance of hope in a vulnerable place.

Now faith is the assurance of things hoped for, the conviction of things not seen. (Hebrews 11:1)

I will stand in faith, having hope that these waves of grief will pass. I will rest in your harbor of hope, knowing that Jordan is happily in your arms. When I don't have enough hope to take a step forward, I will fall forward in faith, knowing you will catch me. My hope is not what is in this world, my hope is wrapped up in you.

For my King to hold my face when I finish my race as Jordan did, and for him to say to me, "I saw every tear that rolled down these cheeks; I know every sorrow that traced this face"—that is my hope that I will hold onto.

Why Didn't You Heal Him?

Why didn't you heal Jordan? I get this question from a lot of people who watched Jordan die and loved him very much. I understand why people ask this question.

When we had Jordan's memorial service, people wanted to offer health suggestions and remedies, but I knew deep in my heart that they were trying to reconcile in their own hearts why Jordan wasn't healed. We know you are a good God and we know you can do miracles. I believed that I was going to see one of those miracles. But you didn't heal him on this side of heaven. I have found the answer to this question is resting in the peace that your ways are so much higher than my ways. I wish Jordan was still here, but I also know that heaven is so much better than living here on earth. How could I wish for Jordan to remain living here in this fallen world filled with sin and pain when he could be whole and well and free in heaven with you?

I know you are doing something bigger than what I can see. You have new things that you are planning and hidden things I do not understand. I rest in your all-knowing power and wait for the new things you are bringing forth in my life.

My hope doesn't cease if I don't receive a healing miracle. My hope doesn't fade when I bury my spouse and close the casket. My hope is all the more renewed, because when I didn't receive that healing miracle, Jordan was swept up in your arms, and he will never see a day of pain again. When I closed the casket and buried my husband, my hope was strengthened even more knowing that he is not under the ground, but he is with you.

"You have heard; now see all this; and will you not declare it? From this time forth I announce to you new things, hidden things that you have not known."
(Isaiah 48:6)

First Time to Do Something My Loved One Always Did

I've been avoiding this household chore, but I know I need to get it done.

Today is the day I am going to replace the kitchen lightbulb. It is a bulb in the light fixture I don't know how to take apart, but I am going to figure out how to do it and replace it myself. This may sound silly, but changing this lightbulb was something I never had to think about when Jordan was alive. It was always the chore he took care of for me and I honestly never thought twice about it. Until now. Why do I feel so emotional about changing a lightbulb?

I had gone to the local hardware store to get the specific bulb I needed when I was suddenly struck with an overwhelming wave of grief—it was like a grenade of grief exploded and I had nowhere to seek refuge. The damage hit me when I got to the bathroom fixtures section. There I was, in the middle of the aisle, just trying to find this stinking lightbulb I need for my kitchen, when I burst into tears. It was pretty ridiculous. Then I saw it: a row of newly arrived handicap-accessible bathtubs. Instantly I was taken back to a time when I came here to check the pricing of these bathtubs for Jordan. I remembered trying to figure out how we could install one of the tubs before Jordan made it home from the hospital. I didn't want him to have to worry about it.

I tried to hide my sobs but then I snapped out of it and asked myself, "How am I here in the bathtub section when I'm trying to find a lightbulb?" I wiped my tears and took a deep breath and chuckled. That was unexpected.

I got the lightbulb and headed home. When I got home to start this simple process, I was again overcome by grief, this time in the form of anger. I am mad that I have to do this by myself. I'm angry that Jordan isn't here to take care of this for me. I am mad at myself for even being angry about this. But mostly, I am mad that he is gone forever.

Will these moments ever get any less difficult? Will there be a time I can change a lightbulb without it being an emotional ordeal?

Hear my cry, O God, listen to my prayer; from the end of the earth I call to you when my heart is faint. Lead me to the rock that is higher than I, for you have been my refuge, a strong tower against the enemy.

(Psalm 61:1–3)

You make me strong when I am weak—even when my weak moments are as silly as an unexpected breakdown at the hardware store, or an outburst of rage while changing a lightbulb. You hear my cry and you know my frustrations. When a grief grenade explodes in my face, you lead me to a place of refuge. When I am fighting a wave of sorrow, you come running to me. You scoop me up in your arms and shield me like a strong tower in the midst of an outbreak of grief.

Am I Having a Faith Crisis?

Something is very different about me now that Jordan is gone. Something strange. I see life in a different way. Sometimes I don't even recognize my own voice or my own thoughts. I noticed this new perspective of mine come out in the way I talk to people, the way I think about life, and the way I plan for the future. Sometimes I feel like I am the only one in the room with my head in the clouds, thinking about what it must be like to be in heaven. It is strange how grief interacts with the mind.

When Jordan took his last breath, I kissed his forehead and asked you to help me reconcile what I had just seen. I did not know how to process my faith after seeing my husband die. I asked you to completely rebuild my theology, because everything I thought I knew about you seemed to not be true.

My faith has gone through several phases. At times I am ignited with hope, but there are times when I feel as though there is no reason for our pain. But you, the God of all comfort, have held my heart through every wave of disbelief that has washed over me. You have whispered hope into my soul and I see you piecing together what is left of my shattered life.

After Jordan died, I read seven books about heaven in forty-eight hours. I wanted to know what Jordan was doing without me. It is such a strange feeling having someone who was once part of you dwelling in the fullness of heaven. Part of my heart feels like it is in heaven too.

I feel like I can't afford to not have faith in you right now. The only hope I have for Jordan is tangled up in what I believe about you and that I believe he is in heaven. But my faith is still wavering at knowing if you are good and if I truly believe you can take this cup of grief from me.

I lift up my eyes to the hills. From where does my help come? My help comes from the LORD, who made heaven and earth. (Psalm 121:1,2)

When I am plagued with these questions of faith, there is only one thing I know to do. I will look to the horizon when my heart is heavy and my head is weary. I will look to the horizon when I am helpless and afraid. I will look to the horizon when I see nothing but hopelessness before me. I will look to the horizon when I'm not able to dream. And I will see my help coming to rescue me. My help is from the Maker of the universe, and he is coming to save me.

To you I lift up my eyes, O you who are enthroned in the heavens!
(Psalm 123:1)

When I am unable to reconcile what is happening here on earth, I will look to you for my peace. Though I am wrestling with knowing if you are still good and faithful, I know you will be the first one to my side holding me when I feel too weak to stand on my own. I will run to you with my questions, knowing that you are not disgusted by my doubts. I will take my doubts, my lack of faith, and my heartache to your throne. You will not overlook my battle. You walk me through every question and misgiving, showing me your faithfulness. When I start to doubt, I will go to your Scriptures to remind me that you have restored hopeless situations before and you will do it again. When I am too weak to have faith, you plant your seed of hope in my heart to keep me breathing.

I know even your disciples struggled with doubt, yet you did not abandon them. I know that you will not abandon me. This season of wrestling in my faith will be a cornerstone of developing my theology. When I start to have questions or doubts, pursue my heart, Lord, and remind me to bring these thoughts to you. You will not silence my struggles, you will tenderly minister to them.

How Can I Suffer and Still Believe in God?

I think the saddest moment in someone's life can often be the most fearful moment of one's life. But with Christ, this very same moment can also be memorialized as the moment you felt the most tangibly near. At least that is the way it was for me.

I can't explain how, in a single moment, I have simultaneously felt the gut-wrenching fear, drowning sorrow, and the ever-present comfort of God as thick and as sweet as honey, all while holding the hand of my dying husband. That is the power of Christ. We carry a lantern of hope that will never snuff out as we trek through the volatile waves of this broken and sin-ridden world. We experience the woes of the world while we wait to be reunited with our King. We hold the hope of the cross in one hand and the pieces of our broken heart in the other knowing that somehow, some way, this absolute wreck of a situation will be reconciled in the hands of the one who mends broken hearts, bad endings, and shattered dreams.

Yes, I will suffer in this life and, yes, I will see miracles in this life. These two juxtapositions will occur all throughout my time here on earth, but what keeps me from being tossed overboard during the unpredictable storms of life is this: my hope in Christ.

> *So when God desired to show more convincingly to the heirs of the promise the unchangeable character of his purpose, he guaranteed it with an oath, so that by two unchangeable things, in which it is impossible for God to lie, we who have fled for refuge might have strong encouragement to hold fast to the hope set before us. We have this as a sure and steadfast anchor of the soul, a hope that enters into the inner place behind the curtain.*
>
> (Hebrews 6:17–19)

There was never a promise that this life would be easy, but you did promise you would be near us when we walk through suffering. That doesn't make you less powerful, but more extraordinary; for you do not shy away from my pain, but rather, you run to it with open arms ready for rescuing.

I will suffer. I will see miracles. But my unchanging God will always be right by my side as my refuge, your hope an anchor for my soul in the raging seas of life.

I Am Afraid to Have Faith Again

It was crushing to hear the news. The doctor came in and didn't even make eye contact with us. I don't think he could. After seeing Jordan's grim results from the scans, how could he look into a young man's eyes full of life and hope and tell him he is dying? The cancer had come back, and it was everywhere.

But I believed.

I believed in my heart that you would heal him. The tumors grew before my very eyes. Jordan's health declined quickly and gruesomely. He lost his vision, his mobility, his voice. More baffled doctors. More horrifying scans.

But I believed.

Doctors from all over the nation told us there was nothing they could do to help us, but I still thought you were going to save us. Jordan never got angry with you. He never lost hope.

But then, he died.

I don't like where I am now. This constant feeling of impending fear expecting that something bad is about to happen is no way to live my life. The only thing I will risk is getting my hopes crushed again, but I can barely stand the idea of that. However, there is another option. What if I go for it, and have faith that everything will be all right, and it actually does end up being all right? It seems risky, to put my hopes in such a vulnerable state, but doesn't this outweigh the benefits that, by some miraculous grace, you do intervene on my behalf? What if something good does happen to me? Maybe you do have good things in store for me after all. Then I would look back at disbelief and see that I have wasted all this time being afraid.

Therefore, I will make my prayer like the apostles:

The apostles said to the Lord, "Increase our faith!" And the Lord said, "If you had faith like a grain of mustard seed, you could say to this mulberry tree, 'Be uprooted and planted in the sea,' and it would obey you."

(Luke 17:5,6)

You will take the mustard seed of faith I have left and make it blossom into a mighty work of your hands. Your grace covers my unbelief. I am realizing that you are the one who uses miracles to grow the mustard seed into flowering fields of faith.

It's scary, but what do I have to lose? I'm going to do it. I'm going to dare to believe again.

I Don't Know if I Believe in Miracles Anymore

A lot of people have been asking me if I still believe in miracles. Since so many people were praying for a miraculous healing for Jordan's life, it is a regular question I am asked. It's one of the first questions I asked you about after he died. Let's not forget I was the leader of it all, praying rigorously for him to live—even after death. I knew he was going to live; I was thoroughly convinced in the depths of my soul that he was going to be healed. But he still ended up dying.

I empathize with this question on so many levels. I feel like this is something I would still be struggling with too, if by your grace, you hadn't wrapped my heart in your promises.

In response to this question, I have to ask myself: Have I forgotten the miracle of a virgin birth to the Savior of the world? What about the resurrection from the grave, where you rose from death three days after being publicly crucified? Have I forgotten the miracle of marriage, where two separate people become one in spirit and in flesh through the covenant of God? Have I forgotten my own salvation, where you drastically made my heart of stone into a heart of flesh?

I didn't see Jordan's tumors go away. I never saw his spine healed or his sight restored. I watched his body fade away, every single day, while he was still trapped in it.

But that is not where his story ends.

So we do not lose heart. Though our outer self is wasting away, our inner self is being renewed day by day. For this light momentary affliction is preparing for us an eternal weight of glory beyond all comparison, as we look not to the things that are seen but to the things that are unseen. For the things that are seen are transient, but the things that are unseen are eternal. (2 Corinthians 4:16–18)

Though I saw his earthen vessel of a human body slowly fade away into dust, I saw his spirit rise, becoming stronger and stronger day by day. His inner strength, endurance, hopefulness, abundant graciousness, and his continued posture of victory always astounded me. He was a vessel reflecting your goodness, and when I looked at him, I could see you. In fact, Jordan's spirit was so strong in you that I did not even realize how deteriorated his physical appearance looked to other people until I saw the shocked face of a visitor who came by to see Jordan. As he took one step closer to heaven, he was taking one step out of the wreckage of his body. You strengthened him from within, and I was able to witness what your strength looks like when glorified through our weaknesses.

For this very reason, I can't *not* believe in miracles. I did witness a miracle. I watched Jordan leave this broken world and enter into eternity.

What Is the Point of Prayer?

I counted the days I slept in a hospital chair instead of a bed while being married to Jordan. It was over three months total. Those nights I slept in hospital chairs I was surrounded by ICU beeps and whistles, muffled moans and stuffed sobs, and whispers of tense conversations from outside our room. Those were the loneliest and scariest nights. I felt powerless and afraid, so I would do the only thing I knew I could do: pray.

I would pray through Scripture, I would pray while crying, and I would sing my prayers over Jordan while he was sleeping. I would even walk down the hospital corridors and pray over patients' rooms. I would beg and plead, proclaim and praise. I would pray for hours and hours into the night, and many a time I never slept, just prayed. I can honestly say that I lived with a prayer on my breath at every moment of every day. I was in desperate need to be in constant communication with you.

Where did that prayer life go? I haven't actually had a proper prayer to you in months. I used to live in prayer. Now I will say an occasional prayer here and there, when socially prompted or asked. But it is nothing like where I used to be in my prayer life. I am really ashamed to admit this. It's not like I purposely stopped praying, I just…stopped. Sometimes I feel like prayer does not really work. I mean, I did the whole "pray without ceasing" thing and Jordan still died.

So, what is the point of prayer? I know I still desire it. I still desperately want to be in communication with you.

> "Now, O LORD, please remember how I have walked before you in faithfulness and with a whole heart, and have done what is good in your sight." And Hezekiah wept bitterly. And before Isaiah had gone out of the middle court, the word of the LORD came to him: "Turn back, and say to Hezekiah the leader of my people, Thus says the LORD, the God of David your father: I have heard your prayer; I have seen your tears. Behold, I will heal you." (2 Kings 20:3–5)

I have limited myself from fully experiencing the richness of prayer. And even more sadly, I have put your character in my manmade box, putting a cage on what our conversations need to look like, and limiting my expectations of your mighty hands. I have only restrained myself from fully experiencing the endless bounds of your love. It's as if I am too afraid to show you all the darkness I am feeling. I cut off our relationship by not coming to you with the messiest of my brokenness. But now is the time I need you most.

My prayer life may look a little different than it used to, but I know I can still run into the same loving arms that never abandoned me. You bend your ear to hear my heart and help me through my wrestlings.

Even though my voice is shaky, and I am questioning your sovereignty, you love on me with your peace. When I am lying on the floor of my closet crying out to you in shock, you hold me through my sobs. When I spit words of doubt and blame at your character, you lean in closer to me and remind me of the truth. When I am begging you to take this cup of pain from me, you send your angels to strengthen me. Prayers don't need to be polished and rated PG. Prayers do, however, always need to be at the same place—tangled up in your unwavering arms.

Prayer is so much more than what I have painted it to be. I have shallowly defined prayer as a genie-in-a-bottle's "your wish is my command!" But no, prayer is so much more than that.

When I limit prayer to ask-and-receive, I miss the depths and beauty of drawing closer to you. I put a box on our intimacy when I view prayer as a disappointment because my request was not met. That doesn't make prayer powerless, it makes prayer all the more powerful because you have torn the veil so that I may go directly to you—with my tears and all of my heart's troubles.

Ungodly Anger?

I'm going to be very honest with you, God. I don't understand why you let this happen to me. In fact, I don't understand why I was led to believe that healing was an option for Jordan when it wasn't. The memories of Jordan's non-functioning limbs and him gasping for air at the very end are ones I just can't seem to shake. How does this reconcile with my faith?

I realize it is ironic for me to be telling you that I am so angry about what happened to me that I do not know if you are even real anymore. Obviously, I must have a glimmer of faith deep down in my soul for me to be crying out to you in the first place. I know in my heart that you are in control. You are the very thing I need right now, and you are also the only one I'm angry at. But if I were to not believe in you, then I would have no one to talk to about my heartache. Therefore, I have to believe in you. Otherwise, I am utterly alone.

I don't want to stop believing in you. If you are not real, then that means Jordan is not with you, his body well and fully restored in the safety of your arms.

On another twisted tangent, my only option to get me out of this pit of grief is to believe in you. You are the only one who could possibly carry me through this. My closest relatives can't because they are also grieving, and my more distant friends can't because they did not know Jordan at the same level of intimacy I knew him.

Quite frankly, I have tasted and seen your good works. Even though I am mad at you right now, I cannot deny that truth. After tasting and seeing that you are good, I could never go back to anything less than the never-ending love that you supply for us who are broken. I feel like a shattered mess on the floor of your throne room. The only one I know who will scoop my pieces off the floor is you—the king, sitting on the throne. I crumble before your feet, and in all your majesty and holiness, you step down from your throne to sweep me up in your arms.

You've been the only one who can handle these angry bouts of mine. You're the only one who doesn't grimace or shrink back in awkward discomfort with my grief-stricken words of anger and shock.

You are the only one who can take it. In your vast power and might, you bend your ear to my harsh lines I hurl at you, embracing me all the more tightly as I shake and cry in anger.

This isn't something you haven't seen before. This anger I have is not something you are silent about in Scripture. Despite my pout, I can't help but admire you all the more for your relentless pursuit of my heart.

I can relate with Jeremiah's anger in Scripture:

Cursed be the day on which I was born! The day when my mother bore me, let it not be blessed! (Jeremiah 20:14)

Jeremiah's rage doesn't end here. He continues to pout, throw a temper tantrum, and complain. But you don't correct him when he curses the day he is born. You don't run away, and you don't even shock him with thunder bolts (although you could). In all your holiness and omnipotence, you do not need a single soul to justify the works of your hands.

I don't need you to justify your actions to me either. I just need you. And you are the first one to my side when I am angry with you. What kind of a God are you? To my human ears, it is absurd to hear how gracious you are to those who are hurting. You created all my emotions in the first place. You fear nothing. Anger doesn't scare you away(even though I've accidentally scared a few innocent bystanders away with my colorful rants).

When it comes down to it, I'm so angry with you I just desperately need you to hold me. It doesn't matter where I am, you calm the raging seas of my soul with one touch from your gentle hand.

"The LORD your God is in your midst, a mighty one who will save; he will rejoice over you with gladness; he will quiet you by his love; he will exult over you with loud singing." (Zephaniah 3:17)

A mighty God who rescues the enraged widow? It seems this couldn't be true. But then you sing over me and quiet my sobbing rants with your unconditional love. This is who my God is. The only way to console the anger I feel toward you is for me to be tangled up in you, with the rage of my heart surrendered at your feet.

Anger can quickly lead to sin; but anger is still an emotion you created. What other God in this universe consoles me while I cry out to him in anger? We can righteously engage in anger by submitting this emotion to Christ—or we can sit in our rage until it becomes bitterness, hard-heartedness, and even apathy.

In my grief, I may feel anger, but I can submit this emotion to you, and wrestle with my disappointments before you. We can sin in our anger or righteously engage in our rage by submitting it to you. I will give you my everything—including my anger. I will submit my anger to you, knowing you will heal my brokenness.

I Feel Like You Owe Me an Explanation

I sat holding Jordan's hand in the ICU room while we waited for our oncologist to give us the news. Our doctor was compassionate and kind, and we knew we were in good hands. I saw him make his way toward our room, but I noticed he couldn't make eye contact with me. I swallowed hard. He came into the room and sat down.

"There's nothing we can do," he told us. As he delivered this message I saw his knuckles become white as they grasped his clipboard.

"What about organ donors?" I asked.

"I'm so sorry, but...his heart could not withstand the stress of such a big surgery."

"What about clinical trials?"

"The tumors are everywhere. There are too many places that need treatment; it would be of no use."

I sat in silence.

I knew I was grasping for straws. I was desperate for anything to save my husband's life. We had already tried every treatment ever invented. After the oncologist made sure I had asked all of my questions, his jaw clenched, and he exited the room quickly. I heard sobbing outside my door. I felt loved that our doctor cared for Jordan so much. I wanted to join him. But I refused to give up.

This memory is painful. But what makes these memories sting even more are the spurts of "healing" laced throughout Jordan's battle with cancer. There were so many moments when we thought he was being healed. What about that time when the emergency room technicians took a look at his scans and announced that they couldn't find any more tumors in his body? Or the time the swelling in face went down overnight? What about the time he started moving his paralyzed legs against all medical odds? Looking back, these moments were such a tease.

I can empathize with Job, when he is crying out to you after losing his property, his children, and his health.

"For the thing that I fear comes upon me, and what I dread befalls me. I am not at ease, nor am I quiet; I have no rest, but trouble comes."
(Job 3:25,26)

Job crying out to you and lamenting his own birth shows me something about your love that I have never fully grasped until now. You can handle the wild emotions of my brokenness.

When I doubt your goodness and blame your perfect character, you still show grace to me and love me still. You are all-knowing and all-powerful, and you do not owe me an explanation for anything you do here on this earth; but in your grace and mercy, you console my temper tantrums and love me with a never-ending grace.

In your lovingkindness, you still restore everything Job has lost and multiply his riches abundantly—even after he questions your goodness. Job realizes that you are perfect and all powerful, and he is not. This realization transforms his heart in the midst of his suffering. His tone completely shifts as he is awestruck by your sovereignty:

"I know that you can do all things, and that no purpose of yours can be thwarted. 'Who is this that hides counsel without knowledge?' Therefore I have uttered what I did not understand, things too wonderful for me, which I did not know."
(Job 42:2,3)

I may never fully understand why Jordan had to suffer the way he did, but I trust you with my life; I know you are doing something better than what I can see. Jordan is with you. Being with you is the ultimate prize we are all living for.

You do not owe me an explanation. If I spend my time chasing down answers and seeking justice for a fight that is not my own, I'm still left on this side of heaven without Jordan. I, like Job, can never fully understand what all you are doing in my life—and in other people's lives.

Lord, I don't need an answer. I don't need an explanation. I desperately need you.

Why Do We Suffer?

There has been one question I have wrestled with while Jordan was suffering, and I continue to wrestle with it even after he died. This question is one I know I will always struggle with, and it's the same question my mentors and pastors continue to wrestle with as well: why do we suffer?

I know some suffering is a natural result from sin. But what about the people who use their dying breaths to praise your name?

Jordan's suffering did not seem fair, but did criminal torture and slow and public execution of an innocent Messiah seem fair?

The answer everyone seems to go to is, "Well, we are in a fallen world." But honestly, this answer just doesn't cut it for me. There is so much more beauty that has come from my ashes and from Jordan's legacy to simply chalk it all up to the fallen world. The enemy doesn't deserve that kind of credit. What I have witnessed through my suffering and experienced through bloody hands and tear-filled eyes has shown me so much more than just a fallen world. I have seen the ever-present hand of God in every detail—every tear drop, every bad report, and every loving nurse. Suffering has been so much more for me than just suffering. I have seen the tenderness of God's children, hurting with me and standing with me in faith. I have seen the unity prayer brings, when meeting people who tirelessly prayed for us for the first time, but feeling like we have known each other for eternity. I have seen reconciliation and forgiveness because where suffering is involved, it is easier to lay down quarrels from the past.

Suffering has shown me that there is so much more to this life than our temporary residence on this planet. I never knew I could be in awe of God while feeling immense brokenness in the midst of suffering.

I'm not a hopeless victim to whatever the world wants to torture me with, because I have you. You bought my residency from this fallen world and have given me full citizenship in heaven. I have you as my lantern, guiding me through this darkness. I am still hurting, I am still missing Jordan, and I still have no idea why I had to watch my husband die, but I have never felt closer to you. Yes, we live in a fallen world. But Jesus, I have you to pull me through it.

For you will not abandon my soul to Sheol, or let your holy one see corruption. You make known to me the path of life; in your presence there is fullness of joy; at your right hand are pleasures forevermore.
(Psalm 16:10,11)

Am I Making Any Progress Through the Grief Cycle?

I am sitting alone in my bedroom waiting for a call back from a relative. She missed my call. For the normal person, this is not a big deal. I know she is at work, and I know she has a ton of meetings today. But I can't help thinking she may be dead somewhere, or in danger. I know in my brain this thought is irrational, but it's the natural response my mind jumps to these days. After so many doctor appointments with medical professionals telling me the scariest news I could ever imagine, I guess it psychologically trained my mind to expect the worse. The one thing I believed would not actually happen—Jordan dying—happened. I feel like I have been trained to expect the worse-case scenario in everyday circumstances.

But today, I couldn't help being a little bit proud of myself. Instead of pacing frantically while clutching my cell phone, I made the intentional decision to set my phone down in my bedroom to go outside and take a walk.

While I was walking, I started talking to you about how annoyed I am with myself for being so afraid and pessimistic all the time. You would think Jordan had died yesterday with all the drama I put myself through! I feel so defeated and frustrated with myself that I am not further along in this journey of grief (and by further along I mean operating like a "normal" person—no more irrational bouts with fear, no more crying, no more of this gloominess).

I used to consider myself a pretty happy person before all this happened; I took joy out of celebrating things, I loved life, and was so stinking optimistic. But lately, I have been the weepy, pessimistic girl in the room. Sporadic crying, the silent person in the group, the bearer of unfortunate news. I am the girl you don't want to emcee your event—I'll either end up crying or telling everyone a sad story about Jordan. I feel like if I take two steps forward in my journey of grief, I wake up crying the next morning and fall five steps behind. Am I making any progress at all? Some days I feel like I am starting all over again, and I am even more sad than I was when Jordan first died.

But you reminded me of some little victories I have had in the past year. For example, I used to not be able to drive by Jordan's old work building; I would do everything I could to take the long route home. Now I have no problem at all driving by there, and I have even gone into the building a few times!

Today was a big victory for me. I took a walk outside instead of incessantly calling my relative until she picked up the phone. My big victories may sound small, but you remind me that you are healing me daily. Some days may look worse than others, while other days will look better than I have experienced in a long time. This does not mean you aren't at work in my life, restoring my heart and healing my brokenness. This only shows me how much I need you daily in order to get through this journey of grief.

Why are you cast down, O my soul, and why are you in turmoil within me? Hope in God; for I shall again praise him, my salvation and my God.
(Psalm 43:5)

Most of the time, I am my worst enemy. I compare myself to myself. This cycle leads to turmoil within me. But Lord, you remind me of who I am to you. You also encourage my soul when I am downcast.

This process of healing is filled with baby steps. We will walk through this journey together, my hand securely in yours. You are guiding me through grief with little victories. These little victories may be a big deal only to us (and I am guessing that it is a big deal to anyone who has checked their missed calls to find 497 messages from a minor panic attack on my end), but you truly are the only one I need in my corner.

I Am Having Trouble Trusting You

I had a harsh realization about the depths of my heart today. I am realizing that my trust in you is severely broken. It took me some time to notice that I had begun to not trust you, first with little things and eventually with bigger things. It wasn't like there was a specific day I remember where I stopped trusting you—it was more like a silent fog that creeps into a bay on a quiet night, slowly settling over the still water and the empty docks.

Learning to live without trusting in you is like learning to live with a gaping wound in my side. I am severely wounded, but not seeking help. Instead I'm living life settling with a gaping wound in my side.

I didn't realize I was not trusting in you until yesterday I heard myself say, "Maybe one day I won't feel this sadness anymore." I then realized other instances where I forfeited my trust in you to the woes of my life. I noticed that I have been living in a closed-off manner, not letting others in too closely, and guarding myself from expecting too much of you.

But we both know how ridiculous this is. Lord, heal my heart of distrust! This is no way to live my life. Lord, will you sustain me as I wait for your mighty hand to move in my circumstances?

For God alone my soul waits in silence; from him comes my salvation.

(Psalm 62:1)

As much as my mind and heart are racing for any sustenance to relieve this empty ache inside my soul, I realize that it is you whom I am waiting for. You are the only one who can console my aches. When you speak to me, my heart's fleeting lies are silenced. I have learned that there are so many times when I think I am waiting on you but, in reality, you are already doing something beyond what I could imagine. Even when "my soul waits in silence" you are saving me.

> *For God alone, O my soul, wait in silence, for my hope is from him. He only is my rock and my salvation, my fortress; I shall not be shaken.*
>
> (Psalm 62:5,6)

When fear grips my shoulders and tries to shake me with anxiety and despair, you rush in and wrap your arms around me, shielding me with your arms, and silencing the lies of the enemy with your words of hope.

> *Trust in him at all times, O people; pour out your heart before him; God is a refuge for us.* (Psalm 62:8)

Is There Any Point to Our Suffering?

What is the point in all this heartache and pain? Will it produce any fruit on this side of heaven? I feel so discouraged about this ongoing pain. Did Jordan suffer for no reason? Am I suffering for no reason?

> *For we do not want you to be unaware, brothers, of the affliction we experienced in Asia. For we were so utterly burdened beyond our strength that we despaired of life itself. Indeed, we felt that we had received the sentence of death. But that was to make us rely not on ourselves but on God who raises the dead. He delivered us from such a deadly peril, and he will deliver us. On him we have set our hope that he will deliver us again.*
>
> (2 Corinthians 1:8–10)

When we are burdened beyond our strength, you are the only one on whom we can rely. You fill our hearts with the hope that can come only from the strength in your arms that carry us through trenches of our trials. Though I may feel like I have received the death sentence on my life, you will deliver me from this hopelessness. Why? Because my hope is set on you.

I have learned a few things about suffering through my journey of grief. I am in a constant position of vulnerability to you. I feel like the only thing I have left to give you is my tears—but you take my tears and transform them into something beautiful.

When we give you our bitter grumblings, you whisper your undeserved grace into our hardened hearts.

When we give you our snuffed-out embers, you breathe hope over the coals of our heart, reigniting our flame for you. When we blame you because of our ignorant and limited perspective, you broaden our horizons by proclaiming the dreams you have for us. When we give you our tainted and untrusting outlook on the bad things that have happened in our lives, you remind us who paid the ransom for our lives to deliver us from the clutches of the evil one.

Whatever I go to you with, whatever I throw your way, you remind me of how good you are and how much I desperately need you. You show me this with the resounding truth that is wrapped up in your unconditional love. You are doing more in my life than what I can see.

Count it all joy, my brothers, when you meet trials of various kinds, for you know that the testing of your faith produces steadfastness. And let steadfastness have its full effect, that you may be perfect and complete, lacking in nothing. (James 1:2–4)

I Don't Feel Like Worshiping You

My heart feels like it is as hard as stone. I am sitting in church during the worship service and I feel absolutely nothing. This used to be my favorite part of Sunday service, and now I dread it. I hate to admit this, but it is almost as if I have no desire to praise you. But I know I am not the only one who has felt this. I am reminded of the Psalms; page after page of raw and vulnerable emotions, written by a psalmist in utter turmoil. I feel like I can relate to every word on these pages.

> *Why are you cast down, O my soul, and why are you in turmoil within me? Hope in God; for I shall again praise him, my salvation and my God.*
>
> (Psalm 43:5)

My pain is great, but my hope in you is greater. Even though I am walking through this season of sadness, I will remember that you are faithful. I will set my eyes and heart on your goodness. I do not understand why Jordan had to die, but I also do not understand the boundless pursuit of your grace and mercy in my life.

Even when I feel too weary to praise your name, you step down from your throne to hold me. In my times of need you have always been there for me. Sometimes I can feel you so close to me it is as if you have a special adoration for me—even when I'm in the depths of despair.

When I'm sitting in church during the worship service and I can't bring myself to stand or sing, I will proclaim your goodness from the depths of my soul. Though I have a shaky voice and snuffled sobs, you will hear the song of my heart. When I feel like I have nothing to offer in praise except my broken heart, I will lift my hands to your heart holding the remaining pieces of my faith for you to restore. When my legs are too weak to stand in hope, I will lean on your strength knowing that you will restore my heart again. When I have no words to say or no song to sing, I will sit at your feet and offer the only widow's mite I have to offer, my tears. And when I feel that sobering stillness of grief that is too deep for words, I will rest at the foot of your throne, soaking in the nourishment of your presence as you till the hardened soil of my heart.

You will always hear my song of worship, even when it is silent or shaky. You bend your ear to hear my heart. You know the hurts I have, the wounds of my soul that still need healing, and the hopes I have lost. However, you are not appalled by my broken state. You scoop me up in your arms and hold me close to your chest. When I am too weak to praise your name, I will rest in your arms as you restore me. When I don't feel like worshiping you, I will point my tear-filled eyes to the cross, and remember that your mercy for me is more than I could ever deserve, and your gracious love for me has no end. For in these times when my heart is in full surrender, I have the sweetest moments of experiencing your comforting presence. I don't have to feel a certain way to know in my heart that you are good. What is the point of worshiping you only when I feel like it? Is that even a relationship? When I don't feel like worshiping you I will worship you even then. You will meet me in my weakness and love me through my pain. This very reason is why I will always worship you.

Do You Hear Me?

I am so moved by your prayer when you were at the Mount of Olives, crying out to your Father in desperation:

And he withdrew from them about a stone's throw, and knelt down and prayed, saying, "Father, if you are willing, remove this cup from me."

(Luke 22:41,42)

You were honest about how you were feeling. You were begging to be delivered from crucifixion. Fully human and fully God, you wrestle at the feet of your Father.

"Nevertheless, not my will, but yours, be done."   (v. 42)

Knowing the journey of suffering you would endure, while bearing the weight of my sin, you still submitted to the plans of God—to save me.

And there appeared to him an angel from heaven, strengthening him.

(v. 43)

And God sent help immediately to strengthen you.

And being in agony he prayed more earnestly; and his sweat became like great drops of blood falling down to the ground.   (v. 44)

I am so impacted by the intensity of agony you felt during this prayer. Your feelings of stress are so intense, your body physically reacted to your emotional pain.

Yet we know this isn't the end of the story.

You endured every lash, every act of torture, intense suffering, mockery, and betrayal. You hung on the tree carrying my curses and shame, so I could be reunited with you.

I know that you hear my cries.

Is It Okay to Feel Sad?

I have always been the cheery, joyful, and goofy girl. But since Jordan died, I feel like a completely different person. It sounds like the understatement of the year, but I am so, so sad. I am sad all the time. I don't want to be this way, but at the same time I feel as if I could burst inside if I don't let myself cry. Is it wrong for me to be sad?

When Jesus saw her [Mary] weeping, and the Jews who had come with her also weeping, he was deeply moved in his spirit and greatly troubled. And he said, "Where have you laid him?" They said to him, "Lord, come and see." Jesus wept. So the Jews said, "See how he loved him!"

(John 11:33–36)

You are not a Christ who overlooks suffering. You are moved by your very spirit when you see our tears.

Then Jesus, deeply moved again, came to the tomb. It was a cave, and a stone lay against it. Jesus said, "Take away the stone." (John 11:38,39)

My Savior, who is all knowing and all powerful, still swoops to my side and weeps with me. You are present in every moment of my grieving, but I know you won't leave me here, just as you didn't leave Mary and Martha to forever weep in despair in front of Lazarus' tomb.

So they took away the stone. And Jesus lifted up his eyes and said, "Father, I thank you that you have heard me. I knew that you always hear me, but I said this on account of the people standing around, that they may believe that you sent me." When he had said these things, he cried out with a loud voice, "Lazarus, come out." The man who had died came out, his hands and feet bound with linen strips, and his face wrapped with a cloth. Jesus said to them, "Unbind him, and let him go." (John 11:41–44)

You hear me, you plead on my behalf, and then, you heal me. You will not leave me here in this season of sadness. This season of mourning is my open invitation to rest in your arms and snuggle into your chest.

When sadness fills my heart, I will cling to your strong arms to carry me. When the sadness in my heart overflows into tears falling down my cheeks, I will shed my tears buried in your loving embrace.

I will place the burden of my sadness at your feet. You will carry me through mourning, but you will not leave me here to be sad forever. I trust that you will heal my heart like you healed Lazarus. But until then, I will let my tears fall in the palms of your healing hands, knowing that not one tear is unseen by you.

Do You Understand How I Feel?

As you suffered on the cross carrying all of my sin and shame, I think of how heaven must have looked away from you suffering and bearing every curse. I imagine all the angels in your kingdom turned their heads away from the sight of the crucifixion because they couldn't bear the sight of you suffering. But God, you looked at your Son, precious and suffering, and made the decision to turn your back on him so he could finish the work that he set out do—sealing my eternity.

In that moment did tears fill your eyes? An all-powerful God choosing not to rescue his own Son? The depths of betrayal you felt I cannot imagine, yet I know you felt my pain as Jordan laid in the hospital bed dying as I stood over him helplessly. My pain is trivial compared to what you bore for me. I know you know my grief.

You never left my side. The God of heaven held my heart as I cried over my loss and held my hands as I walked away from my beloved's body. I will never understand the paradoxical combination of your mightiness and your tenderness, all wrapped in one divine entity.

He was despised and rejected by men, a man of sorrows and acquainted with grief; and as one from whom men hide their faces he was despised, and we esteemed him not. Surely he has borne our griefs and carried our sorrows; yet we esteemed him stricken, smitten by God, and afflicted.
(Isaiah 53:3,4)

You know my suffering. You know my grief. And you have carried mine.

I Am Restless

I cannot tell you the last time I sat down and read an entire chapter of a book, watched a movie, or finished a simple half-hour sitcom. I can't bring myself to sit that long. It's hard for me to even focus or read your Word. But I have noticed that I am constantly doing something. Whether it is out running errands, or redecorating the house, I always have something I need to do. I can't tell you how many times I have redecorated my home and reorganized the furniture.

I easily feel bored with life, and I am ready to get out of town to travel about every two weeks. I wake up early and I go to bed late. I go to bed only when I am about to crash, because I can't emotionally afford lying in bed alone with my thoughts without anything to distract me. If I risk going to bed too early, then I will have to process my thoughts, and processing my current mental state is the last thing I want to do right now. I know I am running away from myself. But I am too busy to think about that right now.

> *Then they cried to the Lord in their trouble, and he delivered them from their distress. He made the storm be still, and the waves of the sea were hushed. Then they were glad that the waters were quiet, and he brought them to their desired haven."* (Psalm 107:28–30)

The storms in my mind are raging, but I know there is only one place I will find rest: in your arms. You will silence the seas of my mind, and calm the waters of my restless heart.

I know that this lifestyle is not sustainable. I also know that what I am doing is not healthy. I am running away from my problems. But here's the thing: no matter how far I try to run from my sadness, it will still be in my heart until I rest in your arms and let you heal me.

Lord, will you turn my restlessness into peacefulness? I am afraid to be still and face what is tumbling around in my mind, but I know your hands are gentle and you will help me process this grief piece by piece, until I am able to sit in your presence and breathe in the healing from your words.

> *"Be still, and know that I am God. I will be exalted among the nations, I will be exalted in the earth!"* (Psalm 46:10)

I Feel Like I Am Getting Bitter

The entangled trap of bitterness is evil and messy. It is bottomless and hopeless. It is toxic to the very soul. Bitterness is the poison that sneaks its way into a wound from a heartache that is in the process of healing. Instead of that wound becoming a mark of victory in Christ, it becomes infected, causing constant pain.

I want to fight the poison of bitterness, but I know that this fight isn't a one-time battle. Slaying the dragon of bitterness is an ongoing, proactive war, dodging the fiery breaths of the dragon with victorious cries of Christ's redeeming power.

When the palliative care nurse came into our unit and told me that this would be the last few hours I had with Jordan, I fell to my knees on that disgusting hospital floor and begged God to spare my heart from bitterness. I asked him to keep my heart soft, that it would never be hardened like Pharaoh's heart.

I knew what I was experiencing was classified as traumatic. I knew that seeing Jordan fight to live would be a vision painted in my memory forever. I knew that watching my sweet husband labor for each breath would break my heart. And I knew that the only one I wanted to hold the pieces of my broken heart after walking down this treacherous path was you.

I look back at that moment where I asked you to spare my heart from bitterness and I can see that you have held my heart every step of the way. Sometimes I can feel little pieces of my broken heart coming back together, as you heal me, day by day.

You see, I know what bitterness can do to the heart. We use the poison of bitterness as a sealant to repair the broken pieces of hearts, piecing them together as an attempt to heal our own grief. We think we are stronger if we can hold on to what happened to us, instead of clinging to the hope of what you brought us through. The temptation to succumb to the lies from the tongue of bitterness is great; it tells me that I am justified in being angry, that I am the victim of a tragedy, and I am dignified in being in despair.

> Remember my affliction and my wanderings, the wormwood and the gall! My soul continually remembers it and is bowed down within me. But this I call to mind, and therefore I have hope:

> The steadfast love of the LORD never ceases; his mercies never come to an end; they are new every morning; great is your faithfulness. "The LORD is my portion," says my soul, "therefore I will hope in him."
>
> (Lamentations 3:19–24)

I Am Feeling Rebellious

I will admit, I am feeling a little rebellious. Jordan faithfully served you with every breath and he still died in pain. Before making decisions, I find myself asking the question, "So what?" After being so close to death, I feel like I have been exposed to the worse-case scenario in every situation. I tried to do everything right, yet there was nothing I could do to stop Jordan from dying. What's the use, anyway?

> *Where shall I go from your Spirit? Or where shall I flee from your presence? If I ascend to heaven, you are there! If I make my bed in Sheol, you are there! If I take the wings of the morning and dwell in the uttermost parts of the sea, even there your hand shall lead me, and your right hand shall hold me. If I say, "Surely the darkness shall cover me, and the light about me be night," even the darkness is not dark to you; the night is bright as the day, for darkness is as light with you.* (Psalm 139:7–12)

The root of my problem is that I am wanting to run away from you. I already feel like you deserted me here alone. You took what I loved from me. But I know I cannot hide from you.

I tried to run away from you, but you still found me. I didn't want anything to do with you—but you didn't care, you just held me while I kicked and screamed at you. I was angry; I even said, "If losing my husband is what it means to be obedient, then I am done!" But you continued to pursue my heart and soften my grip on bitterness. I tried hiding from you, but you still found me. You ran to me and found me. There is no place I can hide from you.

You saved me from myself. Without you, I do not know where I would be. I can try to run away from you, but you will scoop me out of the depths of the mire and cradle me in your loving arms. I can cry, kick, scream, and pout, but you will still surround me with your presence. Nothing will separate me from the depths of your love.

Today Is the Date Jordan Died

I had been dreading today. The first time I walked through the anniversary of Jordan's death was really difficult. The second time, not as bad. However, it is so strange how some years hurt more than the others. As a whole, it does get better as time passes. I need to keep reminding myself of this because it encourages me to keep pressing on.

The night before this date is always daunting. Before I go to bed, I take in a deep breath and pull the covers over my head, praying that tomorrow will be a good day.

When Jordan entered heaven, you sent angels to carry me, love me, hold my head up, and wipe my tears. But how quickly do I forget your astonishing kindness. Last night, after a nice phone call with my best friend, I had the best sleep of the year. My phone was flooded with an abundance of texts, prayers, and prayerful support. My heart is so humbled.

I have noticed that I want to stay busy, and I want to talk about Jordan. I don't want anyone to forget him. I want to be around people who loved him, and I want to hear their memories of his life as well. It is like having little pieces of him that I get to enjoy even though he is not here.

Lord, in all your goodness, you saw this day coming and orchestrated an overwhelming amount of love and support for me. Thank you for every person you sent my way to love on me through today.

This morning, I awoke with a deep sense of joy. It was the first time I have woken up on this day with a deep joy in my heart. I know I have this joy because of the assurance I have that Jordan will never suffer again. The pain he endured here is nothing but a memory to him. I imagine him in heaven running freely, strongly, and boundlessly, on many heavenly adventures and in perfect union with his Creator.

It doesn't mean that there will not be any more pain on this day. I still have heartaches, and I still have excruciating memories. I still have bouts of crippling fear that you are healing in my life. Death is awful. But there is hope.

> Why are you cast down, O my soul, and why are you in turmoil within me? Hope in God; for I shall again praise him, my salvation. (Psalm 42:5)

This hope sustains me and gives me joy when I least expect it, but need it most.

You continue to use Jordan's life as a source of encouragement and of enduring faith to me.

> You have turned for me my mourning into dancing; you have loosed my sackcloth and clothed me with gladness, that my glory may sing your praise and not be silent. O LORD my God, I will give thanks to you forever!
> (Psalm 30:11,12)

I will stand in faith knowing that you will clothe me in gladness. Your glory in my life will overflow into my heart and I will not be able to keep silent—I will be moved to sing your praise.

Today marks the date my husband stepped into his new life with you. Today my husband is walking hand-in-hand with the risen King.

I Am Feeling Weary

I am calling out to you today because I am completely burned out. I have big decisions to make and I feel so weary. I am heavy-laden with burdens and exhausted from grief. Will you come to my rescue and save me?

I am always amazed by how you breathe strength into my lungs when I need perseverance to keep me going. Did I ever lose you? No! I look back at this year and I can clearly see that you were with me every step of the way.

Running this race has left me tired and thirsty, but it won't leave me empty. I may have heartache, but my heart won't always be broken. I may cry down certain aisles of Whole Foods, but my tears will never go unseen by you.

"Come to me, all who labor and are heavy laden, and I will give you rest. Take my yoke upon you, and learn from me, for I am gentle and lowly in heart, and you will find rest for your souls. For my yoke is easy, and my burden is light." (Matthew 11:28–30)

I will march forward in strength, even though right now I feel like I have a limp. I will relearn how to run to the finish line with this new gait. I will rediscover how to live life in this new way, without my other half.

Every piece of me that is missing lies at your feet. You will use my pieces. Nothing will keep these tired eyes of mine from seeing the saving grace of my Savior.

We run to finish the race, but sometimes we show up at the finish line with missing limbs, bandaged wounds, and tattered uniforms. I know when I get to that finish line, everything I ran for will be standing there waiting for me. Jesus, you, in all your beautiful glory, will be standing there waiting for me with open arms. You will wipe the sweat from my brow and kiss the wounds on my feet. You will sweep me up in your arms and carry me home—to my eternal home with you, just as my husband experienced when he finished his race.

My weariness melts away in your presence. You will sustain me to help me keep going.

For I am already being poured out as a drink offering, and the time of my departure has come. I have fought the good fight, I have finished the race, I have kept the faith. Henceforth there is laid up for me the crown of righteousness, which the Lord, the righteous judge, will award to me on that day, and not only to me but also to all who have loved his appearing.

(2 Timothy 4:6–8)

I Am Ashamed of My Grief

It has been over a year since Jordan entered heaven. The first year of grief is filled with countless notes, loving phone calls, and people checking in on how I am doing. The second year, not so much. The griever has officially exited society's grace period for mourning a loved one. Many times, the second year is much more difficult than the first year.

Overall, grief is quite an embarrassing affair. The absentmindedness, impromptu cry sessions, bursts of anger, forgetfulness, and socially awkward encounters can leave any girl feeling in her most vulnerable state.

At the same time, I feel ashamed that I am still not further along in the grief process. I thought after a year was over, I would be back to my happy-go-lucky self. Unfortunately, that is not the case for me. I am still struggling.

> For you formed my inward parts; you knitted me together in my mother's womb. I praise you, for I am fearfully and wonderfully made. Wonderful are your works; my soul knows it very well. My frame was not hidden from you, when I was being made in secret, intricately woven in the depths of the earth. Your eyes saw my unformed substance; in your book were written, every one of them, the days that were formed for me, when as yet there was none of them. (Psalm 139:13–16)

You are not ashamed of me. When I was in my mother's womb, vulnerable and unformed, you had great plans in your heart for me. You loved me then, and you love me now. Though I am a little embarrassed by my current state and season, you are not disappointed in me. You draw closer to me in my shortcomings and you show yourself present in my weaknesses. You have seen me in every state, yet you still say that I am fearfully and wonderfully made. I will not feel ashamed because this is a journey of growth and healing. Every step in grief is a process.

You have seen every part of my human state, yet you are not ashamed of me. Therefore, why should I be ashamed of myself?

I Am Struggling with My Self-Identity

You'd think the last thing I would be concerned about in this wild, rollercoaster ride of grief would be my self-identity. Wrong. Throughout this journey of mourning, I knew some things to expect during the grief process and I worked hard to be self-aware of what I was thinking and feeling so I could healthily process all of my emotions. I wanted to take captive every emotion of grief, surrendering it all to you. I do not want to cage anything up; I know that whatever cycle of grief I suppress now will only come up "bigger and badder" later.

Sometimes, I still struggle with knowing who I am and what I am supposed to do with my life now. I was a full-time caretaker and a newlywed wife. Now I am a twenty-four-year-old widow. Honestly, I don't know what I'm supposed to do with myself in this new stage of life. Today I went to the doctor for a minor checkup. As I was sifting through all the different emotions of simply being in a doctor's office since Jordan died, I was filling out some new-patient paperwork for the appointment. I had to check that little box stating my marital status: "widow." I just sat there, blankly staring at that little checkbox. Widow. Is this who I am now?

> "You shall no more be termed Forsaken, and your land shall no more be termed Desolate, but you shall be called My Delight Is in Her, and your land Married; for the LORD delights in you, and your land shall be married. For as a young man marries a young woman, so shall your sons marry you, and as the bridegroom rejoices over the bride, so shall your God rejoice over you." (Isaiah 62:4,5)

I am more than my marital status. I am more than my loss. When my world is spinning out of control and I don't know which way to go next,

I can remember who you say I am. I am yours. I am chosen by you. I am not forsaken. I am not a desolate wasteland. You take great delight in me.

Even more importantly, I can remember who you are: the rescuing Christ, the saving King, God with us, my ever-present help in time of need, and the Lord of all.

But even you were mocked publicly for your identity.

The soldiers also mocked him, coming up and offering him sour wine and saying, "If you are the King of the Jews, save yourself!" There was also an inscription over him, "This is the King of the Jews." (Luke 23:36–38)

The very inscription placed over your head as you hung on the cross was intended to be a mockery of you, but it is now the truth I proclaim when I am crying out to you to save my life. Your identity is my salvation.

I have been rescued from my own devices, and I am still in desperate need of a Savior. The King of kings hung on a tree for me. I may not know what tomorrow holds, or what I should do with the rest of my life, but I do know this: you will be there with me through every step of the way.

When you look at me, you still see the same girl before Jordan died—your child. Not Mrs. Lewis, or the twenty-four-year-old widow, but your child.

I know who I am in you. Instead of looking to myself for my identity, I will look to who you are and what you have done for me. The only way I will find myself is through you.

Am I Going to Die Now Too?

I had a front-row seat to watching someone die. I never thought I would struggle with the fear of death, but here we are, and I can't say that I haven't been surprised by this whole grieving process.

I am more health-conscious than I have ever been before. I can see that this is becoming an idol I have been chasing for peace.

Being more health-conscious can be a good thing, but I have crossed into the territory of fear, which is not healthy.

We did everything for Jordan. We tried every preventative, every diet, every clinical trial, every treatment, every cutting-edge discovery, every naturopathic regimen, and still Jordan died. How do I know that I am not next? Of course, I would love to be reunited with you in your arms, but I couldn't bear the thought of my family watching me die. This is such a morbid thought, I can't believe it has even crossed my mind—but I am fully aware of the terror and damaging effects the experience I had can leave on a person. I would never wish that on my family.

> For he will deliver you from the snare of the fowler and from the deadly pestilence. He will cover you with his pinions, and under his wings you will find refuge; his faithfulness is a shield and buckler. You will not fear the terror of the night, nor the arrow that flies by day, nor the pestilence that stalks in darkness, nor the destruction that wastes at noonday.
>
> (Psalm 91:3–6)

This thought of dying is a product of fear. Fear is not from you. I am so touched by how you take my fears and transform them into my battle cry of victory. You alone transform my fears into a testimony of your goodness. Your faithfulness is so much stronger than the fears I am tempted to dwell on.

There is so much more at work here than what I fear. Your hand is working in my life. Jordan's death was not a life you just so happened to overlook. Jordan going to heaven does not depict that he was not protected by your wings. You had a plan. I may not know exactly what your plan is, but I can rest in the promise that you will deliver me from the snare of the fowler and cover me in protection. I am not a victim of the evil doings of the enemy. I am your child who is used for your magnificent glory. I am protected by you.

You are in control and you are good.

I Feel Helpless

I feel helpless in two ways: I feel like I don't have any control over my life, and I feel like I can't climb out of this trench of sadness. It is like I am tossed around by the winds, hoping to land somewhere in your serene green pastures. I do not know what is going to happen next in my life, and at the same time, I do not know if I will burst into tears in the next ten minutes. It is extremely uncomfortable feeling this helpless. This helplessness to feel better or to get better is quite frightening for me. There is no "Ten-Day Fix" to kick grief to the curb for good. Wouldn't that be nice!

Am I the only one who feels this way? There must be someone else out there who understands what I am feeling.

Be gracious to me, O Lord, for I am in distress; my eye is wasted from grief; my soul and my body also. For my life is spent with sorrow, and my years with sighing; my strength fails because of my iniquity, and my bones waste away. (Psalm 31:9,10)

David is in complete distress. He doesn't know what tomorrow will look like or what the years to come will hold. Running from King Saul who wants to kill him, David cries out to you. A huge bounty on his head and a king on his tail, David runs from Saul for seven years. Seven years of helplessness! Yet he cries out to you in his despair and you listen to him.

Blessed be the Lord, for he has wondrously shown his steadfast love to me when I was in a besieged city. I had said in my alarm, "I am cut off from your sight." But you heard the voice of my pleas for mercy when I cried to you for help. (Psalm 31:21,22)

You alone are my help in time of need. You will wondrously show your steadfast love to me.

Will there be a time when I can get out of this? The answer is yes. Like you restored David to king, and protected him from the jealous hands of Saul, you will deliver me from this season of darkness. You not only gave David peace when he was in hiding and completely helpless, you drew him out of his season of darkness, restoring his life. I am not helpless, but helplessly surrendered in the palms of your hands.

When I feel helpless, I am that much more stronger in you, because I am depending on you to fight for me. The truth is, I am helpless without you. But you fight my case for me when I surrender my burdens to you. My weakness is hidden in the might of your victorious hands. I may feel helpless, but I am not hopeless. My fight is being won by you.

I Am Experiencing Anxiety

I may sound crazy, but I have a weird feeling of fear deep in my gut. There is no particular reason for this feeling, and I can't identify why I feel afraid, but it's there and I can't figure out the root of it. I feel like I have a million valid reasons to feel anxiety, but not one is particularly standing out.

Honestly, anything future related is overwhelming and daunting in my mind—I have made future plans before and they have been shattered. It's scary to even attempt to think about the future right now; every time I do, I have trouble breathing. My heart pounds loudly as if it is in my ears, and sometimes I feel short of breath, even if I am sitting.

Anxiety is no joke. I am so thankful for my counselor who helped me identify that I was struggling with anxiety and panic attacks. I have a friend and a mentor I can talk to when I start to feel anxious, and it helps me recognize the root of the fear and calm down.

Anxiety is such a slippery slope. There are so many levels and layers of this type of fear. Sometimes if I think too much about having anxiety, then I start feeling—you guessed it—anxious.

This feeling of anxiousness comes sneakily in the night before I fall asleep, or peers over my shoulder while I am driving in traffic. It paralyzes my rational thinking when I am faced with big decisions or makes me feel overwhelmed when I am in a large crowd. Sometimes, I don't even know the cause of this feeling of fear.

The wilderness and the dry land shall be glad; the desert shall rejoice and blossom like the crocus; it shall blossom abundantly and rejoice with joy and singing. The glory of Lebanon shall be given to it, the majesty of Carmel and Sharon. They shall see the glory of the LORD, the majesty of our God.

Strengthen the weak hands, and make firm the feeble knees. Say to those who have an anxious heart, "Be strong; fear not! Behold, your God will come with vengeance, with the recompense of God. He will come and save you." (Isaiah 35:1–4)

I know you are near me when I am feeling anxious. While my heart is on the mend, you hold me through those sleepless nights and sing your song of peace over me until I am able to breathe again. You will seek vengeance on the fear that tries to cripple me. When I feel like anxiety is chasing me, you will chase after me with a pursuit that is more tenacious than my own fear. You not only bring me peace, but your righteous hand calls out the cause of my fear and seeks vengeance on behalf of my despair. You protect me. I am not a victim of fear. You will come to save me.

I Am Nervous About My First Counseling Appointment

I know I need to do this, but I am so nervous about it. Today is my first counseling appointment. I was advised early on that this is a healthy and wise decision to make while going through grief. But I can't help wondering: will they tell me I am really messed up? Because if they tell me I am going insane, I am not sure how much more bad news I can take at this point. What if my counselor tells me that I am a hopeless case? I do not want to be nervous but I am.

Counseling appointments are scary for several reasons:

First of all, I do not know the person to whom I am confiding my secrets. I am not sure if I will trust them.

Second, I do feel pretty insecure about my current state of mind. What if my counselor judges me or tries to discipline me?

Thirdly, I do not want to be misunderstood. I feel like I am misunderstood enough already in this life; it would be rather frustrating if I had to pay someone to professionally misunderstand me. Just to be honest.

My fourth point is self-admittedly rooted in insecurity. What if my counselor tells me that I am a hopeless case? I mentioned this before, but any bad news about any type of health-related issue for me is scary. I heard enough bad reports from medical professionals in nine months than most people hear over an entire lifetime. I do not think I can bear another potential bad report at this point in my life.

Lord, I know that you care about my mental health. I also know that this is the right next step for me. I ask that you would use every moment in this counseling session for my edification and for your glory. Lord, please guard my heart and protect me. Help me to articulate what I am thinking and feeling. Guide my thoughts, guide my discernment, and guide my heart. Help me to retain what I need to learn or realize about myself. Thank you for giving me this open door to pursue mental health.

Holy Spirit, let your truth reign in this counseling appointment. Will you speak to me through this time with my counselor? I thank you that you will guide me through this season of healing. Please continue to show me how to seek healing through my grief.

In Jesus name, amen.

"I still have many things to say to you, but you cannot bear them now. When the Spirit of truth comes, he will guide you into all the truth, for he will not speak on his own authority, but whatever he hears he will speak, and he will declare to you the things that are to come." (John 16:12,13)

Here we go!

I Just Had My First Counseling Appointment

I did it! I just completed my first counseling appointment. And surprisingly, it went great! Thank you, Lord, for guiding me to seek counseling. We talked about a lot of things, and they provoked a number of thoughts that I will need to safely process with you.

One thing I think I will need to establish through this journey of counseling is a trusted person with whom I can verbally process what went on in my appointment. I want to make sure this person is someone who will always point me toward Scripture, which I think will help me sort my thoughts and further my healing process.

I was afraid going into this appointment, but I could see that you helped in planning the counselor I was given, and I could see that I really needed to talk to someone.

It was shocking to hear myself talk in my sessions. I had no idea how much I was feeling and how alone I felt in all the different ranges of emotions that are entangled with the grief cycle. I realized that there are a lot of layers of my journey that I have not processed healthily.

I truly believe you entrusted me with this story. I want to steward well the cycle of grief so that I may be used as your vessel to help bring others into healing. I am so thankful that even in a scary first appointment with a counselor, you are with me. I am looking forward to my next phase of healing through this process of grief.

Therefore, confess your sins to one another and pray for one another, that you may be healed. The prayer of a righteous person has great power as it is working. (James 5:16)

Thank you for holding my hand through today.

I Don't Know How to Express What I'm Feeling

Grief is like a thick blanket of fog settling over everything in my life, clouding my discernment in decision-making and covering every way I operate in day-to-day life. I struggle with identifying exactly what I feel and why I am feeling it. Articulating my feelings through this fog of grief seems impossible, and then I feel stuck because I'm not able to identify exactly what I am feeling or how I can get out of it.

I am so thankful that you have given me an inner circle of friends in whom I am able to confide about my heartache. I also praise you for placing professional counselors here on earth to talk to about my grief.

But there are times I feel speechless and I don't know how to talk about what I am feeling. I know I need to, and I want to healthily process this grief, but I don't even know where to start. When I feel lost in the fog of grief, I know where I can be found. I will pour my heart out to you. It is strange because even though I don't know exactly what I am feeling or why I am experiencing what I am feeling, you do, and you show me the way through the fog of grief. You know me and see right through me.

When you went to Jacob's well in Samaria to rest from your travels, you knew what you were doing. I know you didn't sit at that well by chance, for you had a greater plan in mind. You knew a very broken Samaritan woman, tangled up in adultery, would draw her water from the well where you were sitting. You knew she would come in the middle of the day to avoid the judging eyes and harsh gossip of fellow Samaritan women drawing water from the well.

So he came to a town of Samaria called Sychar, near the field that Jacob had given to his son Joseph. Jacob's well was there; so Jesus, wearied as he was from his journey, was sitting beside the well. It was about the sixth hour.

A woman from Samaria came to draw water. Jesus said to her, "Give me a drink." (John 4:5–7)

You ask her for a drink and she is shocked. You are counterculturally initiating conversation with her, revealing your loving heart and relentless pursuit of the lost.

The woman said to him, "Sir, you have nothing to draw water with, and the well is deep. Where do you get that living water? Are you greater than our father Jacob? He gave us the well and drank from it himself, as did his sons and his livestock." (vv. 11,12)

She still has no idea who the Messiah is, yet he initiates conversation with her—a character trait of pursuing the lost.

Jesus said to her, "Everyone who drinks of this water will be thirsty again, but whoever drinks of the water that I will give him will never be thirsty again. The water that I will give him will become in him a spring of water welling up to eternal life." (vv. 13,14)

So many times I do not fully understand the weight of the majesty of who you are. However, my finite human mind does not limit the goodness you show to me. You initiate pursuit of my heart and you initiate conversation with me, even when I am completely oblivious to your holiness and glory.

The woman said to him, "I know that Messiah is coming (he who is called Christ). *When he comes, he will tell us all things." Jesus said to her, "I who speak to you am he."* (vv. 25,26)

Then, you read her mail. You see right through her façade and tell her all the secrets she has buried deep within her heart.

So the woman left her water jar and went away into town and said to the people, "Come, see a man who told me all that I ever did. Can this be the Christ?" (vv. 28,29)

She knew you were the Messiah because you knew her through and through. You did not run away from her secrets, but instead you ran to her. In turn she felt loved, pursued, and awestruck by your goodness.

I am moved to tears reading about the woman at the well, because I know that in this story I am her. My countless sins are all secrets I attempt to hide, yet you still initiate conversation with me. You seek my heart and gently pursue me.

I may not know how to start talking about what I feel or confess the dark secrets that are hidden in my heart, but you still pursue me to bring me into your light.

I will start the journey one conversation at a time. I do not need to worry what you will think because you already know me. I can start with you because you are the safest person in whom to confide. Through these conversations, you will reveal to me all the places where I need you. You will step into my weaknesses and shine your light where I am lost or attempting to hide from you.

Will I Ever Dream Again?

It is very difficult for me to think about my future. I can't help thinking that if I dare to dream again, my hopes will be crushed. I have dreamt before—and I have dreamt wildly! I had a dream to grow old with Jordan, own a spacious home where we could host huge events, and have tons of children. But these dreams seem like they will never happen. When Jordan died, I felt as though my dreams died too.

But I know this is nothing more than a lie from the enemy. You see, I have learned how to properly dream from the one who created dreaming. You have shown me that I can't out-dream what you have planned for my life.

Now Thomas, one of the twelve, called the Twin, was not with them when Jesus came. So the other disciples told him, "We have seen the Lord." But he said to them, "Unless I see in his hands the mark of the nails, and place my finger into the mark of the nails, and place my hand into his side, I will never believe." (John 20:24,25)

Thomas's skepticism cost him eight days of not believing that you were alive. Eight days of hopelessness. Eight days of despair. His doubt didn't protect him, but robbed him of hope, wasting eight whole days of his life when he could have been rejoicing in your resurrection.

Our doubt only causes us to suffer. We miss out on the joy and hope you have in store for us to experience. Thomas cheated himself out of eight days of his joy being restored and his hope resurrected. Like Thomas, I see myself buying into the lie that you are finished with me. But I know that this couldn't be any further from the truth.

Then he said to Thomas, "Put your finger here, and see my hands; and put out your hand, and place it in my side. Do not disbelieve, but believe." Thomas answered him, "My Lord and my God!" (John 20:27,28)

Lord, will you heal my heart from doubting your goodness? I don't want to be like Thomas and miss out on the hope and joy you have for me while I am waiting to see what you will do next with my life.

Though I cannot conjure up enough of my imagination to even begin to restore my broken dreams, you are orchestrating every detail of my life for your glory.

You dream for me when I cannot muster up the strength to dream for myself. Your plans for me are more vast and more beautiful than I could ever hope.

For the LORD comforts Zion; he comforts all her waste places and makes her wilderness like Eden, her desert like the garden of the LORD; joy and gladness will be found in her, thanksgiving and the voice of song.

(Isaiah 51:3)

You Are Doing Something Bigger Than I Can Imagine

When Esther moved in with Mordecai, did she have any idea what her story would look like? She must have thought her life was crashing around her after losing her parents. But little did she know what you had in store for her life.

> *He was bringing up Hadassah, that is Esther, the daughter of his uncle, for she had neither father nor mother. The young woman had a beautiful figure and was lovely to look at, and when her father and her mother died, Mordecai took her as his own daughter.* (Esther 2:7)

Not one detail goes unseen by you. You even used Esther's beauty for your glory. You would take this orphaned little girl and develop her into a queen who found favor in the eyes of the king. You would use her to change history and save the Jews.

> *And when Esther was taken to King Ahasuerus, into his royal palace, in the tenth month, which is the month of Tebeth, in the seventh year of his reign, the king loved Esther more than all the women, and she won grace and favor in his sight more than all the virgins, so that he set the royal crown on her head and made her queen instead of Vashti. Then the king gave a great feast for all his officials and servants; it was Esther's feast.* (Esther 2:16–18)

In every moment of Esther's life, you had a plan. You used what made her different to save your people. In the book of Esther, your name is not mentioned once. But we see the obvious works of your hands all throughout the book. I believe this book is in the Bible to remind us that though we may not see you, or know what you are doing, you are still moving, planning, designing, and orchestrating every little detail of our lives.

Then King Ahasuerus said to Queen Esther and to Mordecai the Jew, "Behold, I have given Esther the house of Haman, and they have hanged him on the gallows, because he intended to lay hands on the Jews. But you may write as you please with regard to the Jews, in the name of the king, and seal it with the king's ring, for an edict written in the name of the king and sealed with the king's ring cannot be revoked."

(Esther 8:7,8)

I do not know what you are doing in my life. But I know that you do not overlook any detail about me. I may not see what you are doing, but that does not mean you are not moving. I will stand in the same courage and confidence you gave Esther. I know that my life is in the hands of the one who writes history, moves mountains, saves his people.

This isn't the end of my story.

First Anniversary I Don't Feel Sad...Is That Bad?

I never knew how much you could heal a person until today.

Today is the first time I have celebrated one of our anniversaries without Jordan that I actually don't feel too bad. I am a little sad, but not to the point where I felt like I couldn't get out of bed this morning. I did my normal routine, and even went and got coffee with a friend this morning. I can honestly say that for an entire hour and a half I did not feel sad. Am I a horrible person? Should I be sad a little bit longer?

It is silly to think that the number of days I grieve Jordan's life mirrors the amount of love I have for Jordan. But I see myself buy into that lie all the time.

My progression through grief is the evidence of your healing hand in my life. The more I move toward my new season of healing and happiness, the more I am able to clearly see your purpose in the time Jordan and I had together. It is interesting how the more joyful I am in heart, the more accurately I am able to remember Jordan for who he truly was. I am able to see him through a lens of joy instead of through the clouded lens of heartache (which tends to memorialize a person instead of realistically celebrating his life).

This day is riddled with memories that I know will never be a real part of this day ever again. They are buried with Jordan. But I am walking through today clothed in your strength.

Today also marks a new memory: the first anniversary I can tangibly see progress toward wholeness in you instead of emptiness in my grief. My cry sessions are half of what they were on this day, and I can't help but feel a deep sense of hope knowing that this day will get easier to endure in the years to come. Happy anniversary to what Christ is doing in my heart!

The moving power of Christ is evident in my life through the trials I have overcome by your healing power. It is limiting to say that I have forgotten Jordan because I am not as sad on our anniversary as I used to be. You are doing so much more in my life. You are restoring my joy and healing my heart—this is a day to celebrate what your resurrecting power is doing in me!

He heals the brokenhearted and binds up their wounds. (Psalm 147:3)

Strength and dignity are her clothing, and she laughs at the time to come.
(Proverbs 31:25)

Should I Move Out or Keep Our Home?

Sitting on the living room floor of the little apartment Jordan and I made our home, I can't help thinking to myself, *If only these walls could talk.* I would journal their stories in hopes to savor every memory that happened inside them.

There are so many memories nestled into every nook and cranny of this apartment, the home that Jordan and I created together. I can almost see him sitting in the corner on the French chair laughing. I see him at the kitchen sink with his apron on, making us hot cocoa before watching a movie. In the bedroom we would stay up watching funny movies and laughing to our hearts' content. This is the first and only home I shared with him. This place is so much more than a living space. It is my home.

But every morning I wake up, I see the empty side of the bed, or the side of the sofa where he used to sit, only without him there. These sweet memories are now a source of pain, rubbing raw my soft heart. But is this holding me back from moving forward?

This is a big decision to make, but I know you will lead me in the ways you have orchestrated for me. This is a decision that can easily become tangled in so many different opinions, memories, and sentimental moments. But if I am completely honest with myself, I know that this home doesn't hold Jordan's memories. I hold the sweet moments I shared with Jordan in my heart, as a gift you gave me. This is a decision that I need to make based on what will best aid in my healing.

Lord, will you guide me in the best decision regarding the home Jordan and I shared? I love this place so much, but I know that what happened under this roof will never be replaced. I know that every moment within these walls was a gift lavishly given to me by your gracious hands. Thank you that this is not the peak of my life. You have more sweet memories for me to delight in, and more adventures ahead for me to conquer. Be near my side, sweet Jesus, as I go through the process of deciding if I should move out of this home or keep it. Thank you for caring about every detail of my life. In Jesus' name, amen.

And he who was seated on the throne said, "Behold, I am making all things new." Also he said, "Write this down, for these words are trustworthy and true." (Revelation 21:5)

What Career Should I Pursue Now?

I have come to a bit of a crossroads in my life, to say the least. Now that I am on my own, I need to figure out what I want to do with my life. I have bills to pay and a lifetime in front of me that will require some sort of income. What career should I pursue now?

I have to be honest, when I first started thinking about the next steps forward in my life I felt very overwhelmed. Asking myself this question is such a strange feeling because it feels like I am starting over. I am a little sad about starting over, but I have come to terms with it, and now it feels exciting. I love the thought of being able to start something new.

I also realize I am a different person. Should I step back into what I have always known, or try a new adventure? I feel like a butterfly in a cocoon, eager to escape this shell, but wanting to be strong and ready for when I first spread my wings to fly.

I think a change of scenery could be really good for me. I also think a new adventure could help redefine myself, even if I am only redefining myself to me. A new career could be a complete disaster, or it could be the best thing to possibly come out of my current life situation. What do I have to lose after all? My life? Been there, done that. (Sorry for the dark humor, I couldn't help myself!)

I am going for it. I am your blank canvas, Lord, ready to be used for your beautiful works. Show me who I am and how you want to use me in this brokenness. There are a few fun jobs I have always wanted to try; why not go for it? There is an exciting opportunity knocking on my door that could completely transform me; what is holding me back? The only thing holding me back from diving into a new adventure is me. I fear that if I move forward, I will leave Jordan behind. I love and cherish the season of being his bride, but I know that I cannot stay in that season forever. I know you have so much more in store for me.

When I think about the different possibilities and the new adventures that await me, I feel excited and afraid at the same time. But when I look to you, I see that your hand has been guiding me since the very beginning, and you will continue to guide me every step of the way. I am not here at this crossroad by accident. You know exactly what you are doing, and you have my next steps planned for me.

So maybe I should rephrase my question: What adventure do you want to take me on next?

Then David said to Solomon his son, "Be strong and courageous and do it. Do not be afraid and do not be dismayed, for the LORD God, even my God, is with you. He will not leave you or forsake you, until all the work for the service of the house of the LORD is finished." (1 Chronicles 28:20)

Will I Ever Love Again?

The sad thing about grieving your husband is that you need your husband to grieve your husband. As C. S. Lewis describes it, when one loses a spouse they become an amputee. We have to relearn how to live life without the other half. It has been awhile since I lost Jordan and quite honestly, I am still learning this new way of living.

Despite the pain of loneliness I am feeling, I can't help wondering if it is possible for me to ever love someone else like I loved Jordan. I am not sure if I am lovable to anyone. I have already been married, and I am worried everyone will take one look at me and see how big of a wreck I am. But I also feel like I was created to love.

The aspect of marriage I miss the most is belonging to someone. At the end of the day, everyone has their person they can go home to. I want to belong to someone, too. I was thinking about why belonging to someone is so important to me. I do feel like I have been tossed out into the world, left to fend for myself. When you belong to someone, they will fight for you, cheer for you, cry with you, and stand in your corner when life gets tough. I feel lost in the wind—aimless, meaningless, and alone. I never had to watch a movie alone, cook for one, or sleep by myself.

But now thus says the LORD, he who created you, O Jacob, he who formed you, O Israel: "Fear not, for I have redeemed you; I have called you by name, you are mine." (Isaiah 43:1)

I do belong to someone. I belong to you. And I have been so comforted by the fact that you have written my name on the palms of your hands. I do not know if I will love again, but I do know the power of your healing hands. My story doesn't end in loneliness because I belong to the author who redeems stories.

For if we live, we live to the Lord, and if we die, we die to the Lord. So then, whether we live or whether we die, we are the Lord's.   (Romans 14:8)

As straightforward as it gets, this verse encourages me. I am yours regardless of what I feel. I will rest in this truth as you guide me through this season of being alone.

What if I Forget My Loved One?

I was clearing out my old voicemails and stumbled across a message from Jordan. I must have listened to it at least twenty times. I had forgotten the sound of his voice and the pattern of his speech. What more will I forget about him? Will I forget the way his eyes shown in the sun or the way he had crinkles around his eyes when he smiled?

I realized today that there may come a time when I start to forget the little things about Jordan. Will I forget the sound of his laugh or the way he would put his hand to his mouth when he was thinking? Will I forget the sound of his footsteps or the inside jokes we shared? I am afraid I will forget more pieces of him because the time we will have apart will be longer than the time we were together.

For the first time this morning, I woke up and Jordan wasn't the first thing on my mind. I didn't realize this until I made my way to the kitchen to make a cup of coffee. Instead of being happy and seeing this as a step forward in the grief progress, I was deeply disturbed. It frightened me. It is sobering to think that someday I may forget all the little things about Jordan. I am afraid he will just become a memory instead of someone I'm living without.

I know that in this fallen world, my heart will experience aches and pains through the stretching that growth brings. Some of this means letting go, and some of this is the natural toll of the world on my human mind. But I have a refuge who will never leave me. In you I always will place my trust. Who else knows the wanderings of my heart? Who else knows the crazy questions haunting the corners of my mind? You know my every thought and you understand my heart's fears.

I don't want to be afraid tomorrow, but I can't help being afraid today. I am fearful that I will forget Jordan. What if I get too happy here without him? Does that mean I am heartless?

But then I'm reassured knowing that Jordan is safely in your arms and he is experiencing the riches of being in your glory. He doesn't miss me; he's full of joy and delight, savoring every moment with you.

For some odd reason, it's really comforting knowing that Jordan does not miss me at all. Time is nothing to him, and time is nothing to you because you are infinite. Today I will write down my sweet memories I have of Jordan. I will probably cry a little bit and then I will get a cup of hot tea and sit in your presence. I will savor the hope I have that I will be reunited with you once again. The more my memories of Jordan fade away, the closer we are coming to stepping into your glory.

For the mountains may depart and the hills be removed, but my steadfast love shall not depart from you, and my covenant of peace shall not be removed," says the LORD, who has compassion on you. (Isaiah 54:10)

My flesh and my heart may fail, but God is the strength of my heart and my portion forever. (Psalm 73:26)

I Am Afraid to Be Happy Again

There is a difference between feeling the depths of joy and feeling happiness. I have joy deep within my heart because I have hope in Christ, but happiness is something I haven't truly felt in a long time. Effortless laughing, lighthearted giggling, carefree smiling, are all lighthearted delicacies in which I wish to indulge. I want to have these back again, but I am afraid if I embrace the happiness you have in store for me, I will be leaving Jordan and all my memories with him behind. If I am happy, does that mean I am cruel and leaving everything I know and loved about Jordan behind?

> But Naomi said, "... Turn back, my daughters; go your way, for I am too old to have a husband. If I should say I have hope, even if I should have a husband this night and should bear sons, would you therefore wait till they were grown? Would you therefore refrain from marrying? No, my daughters, for it is exceedingly bitter to me for your sake that the hand of the LORD has gone out against me." Then they lifted up their voices and wept again. And Orpah kissed her mother-in-law, but Ruth clung to her.
>
> (Ruth 1:11–14)

I can definitely relate with the hopelessness of Naomi. I feel her pain and confusion. However, this is what I know about you—you are a Redeemer. You not only redeemed Ruth's life of sadness, you used Boaz to show how you are our Kinsman-Redeemer. You gave her a family and lineage. You didn't leave her to despair. How could I succumb to the waves of hopelessness when I see how much you have already carefully orchestrated my life? When I think of how Jordan and I met in the first place, that in and of itself was a miracle carefully planned by you.

So Boaz took Ruth, and she became his wife. And he went in to her, and the LORD gave her conception, and she bore a son. Then the women said to Naomi, "Blessed be the LORD, who has not left you this day without a redeemer, and may his name be renowned in Israel! He shall be to you a restorer of life and a nourisher of your old age, for your daughter-in-law who loves you, who is more to you than seven sons, has given birth to him." (Ruth 1:13–15)

You even restore Naomi's life through Ruth's story. You do not overlook any detail. You are the designer of dreams and you are still painting my piece. My script is not over here on earth. You remind me that even though Jordan's life here on earth is over, my life is not over. You reach down into the darkest parts of my mind and shine your light on them. When I am too weak to hope, you strengthen me with your promises.

Embracing happiness means embracing hopefulness. Lord, this is very scary for me. What if I am left even more unhappy and more hopeless? Could you really restore me?

When you redeem broken lives, you use the pieces of our journeys to make an even more beautiful story than before. This is the art of your redemption. I am not leaving Jordan behind, but giving you the pages of my life that are torn so that you can mend my story, writing new chapters and new beginnings. The book of Ruth ends at the beginning of her redeemed life. I know you will rewrite my ending with a happy beginning.

Taking Off My Wedding Rings

"Have you thought about taking off your wedding rings?"

My psychologist's question pounded in my head. What an appalling question. How dare he ask me to consider taking off the only physical evidence I have left to show that I was married to Jordan! But that's just it. I was married to Jordan—but I'm not his bride anymore.

If people see that I'm not wearing my rings, will they think I have forgotten Jordan? Will they think I have moved on? I can't help asking these questions of myself even though deep down inside I know it doesn't matter what anyone thinks. My love for Jordan and my cherished memories of him are not dependent on anyone else's opinions of me. They are far too precious for that. But taking off these rings means I really have to face the fact that Jordan isn't here protecting me, covering me, or loving me anymore. It means I have to grip the reality that he isn't here anymore—and he isn't coming back.

I know this is the next step in my healthy recovery from the loss I experienced. I will take each day step by step. My counselor suggested trying to take off the rings for just a few hours at first, and then gradually building up time without wearing the rings from there.

Though my ring finger is bare, my heart is not. The white crease on my ring finger shows the eternal evidence of a marriage that was rich in love and rich in sacrifice.

"For as a young man marries a young woman, so shall your sons marry you, and as the bridegroom rejoices over the bride, so shall your God rejoice over you."

(Isaiah 62:5)

I loved being Jordan's bride. But now he gets to be your bride. Everything Jordan did to love me well he learned from you, because you are the ultimate Bridegroom. To think that he is in your arms and experiencing what it is like to be a bride—that is priceless for me. You are the creator of love and the author of marriage. I experienced only a taste of what he is experiencing now in your presence. You are the one who showed us how to love in the first place, even when it came to the ultimate sacrifice.

> *"For the Lord comforts Zion; he comforts all her waste places and makes her wilderness like Eden, her desert like the garden of the Lord; joy and gladness will be found in her, thanksgiving and the voice of song."*
>
> (Isaiah 51:3)

It doesn't matter if there is a ring on my finger or not; the only thing that matters is who is holding my hand. Taking this big step forward is so frightening, but I know you will be holding my hand every step of the way. I am even starting to think you had me be the bride of Jordan to show me a piece of who you are as the Bridegroom. And even still, you are immensely more.

Though my covenant of marriage to Jordan is broken, you will never break your undying and unrelenting covenant of love for me.

I will leave my rings on the nightstand. But I know you will hold my heart.

Moving Forward

This morning I woke up with tears on my face. I don't understand why I am walking through this sadness. I don't understand why Jordan had to walk through his pain. But honestly, I don't really need to understand. I don't need answers. I just need you. I have pain and want you to take it.

I know you and I know how wild you have always been—unpredictable and reckless, unable to be tamed. But we all love you like that. We don't always know we love you like that, but we do.

I never want to leave you, God, for apart from you there is nothing. You hold my heart and you are my everything. I couldn't do this without you. Without you, I am nothing—a clanging gong or a resounding cymbal.

I can see that you have given me gifts to grace my journey and guard my heart. In your goodness, you have given me the following gifts:

Faith. You've sovereignly gifted faith to me, and although it hurts to have sometimes, I will never give it up. It has sustained my heart and protected me from bitterness.

Hope. For the mornings when I wake still here on earth, I am able to see you have a reason for me to remain here. Even though I am away from you yet another day, I will continue to wait until I see your face, for it is my greatest desire. I know this isn't my home and it's okay that I feel uncomfortable here without you.

Love. The greatest gift of all. Throughout my journey of grief, you have shown me the boundless depths of your love. Through sleepless nights and painful mornings, you were always by my side.

Thank you for giving me nine months of marriage to Jordan. When his journey here was finished, at age twenty-three, you carried him back to your home. Although my heart was broken, I still knew you loved him more than I did. And I knew you loved me more than I could ever understand.

I do not know all your ways and thoughts, but I have seen your love and faithfulness and I never want to be away from you. I just can't be apart from you. I need you. I have seen the depths of my heart and the unconditional love of yours, and I can see my desperation for you now more than ever.

> O LORD, *you have searched me and known me! You know when I sit down and when I rise up; you discern my thoughts from afar. You search out my path and my lying down and are acquainted with all my ways.*
> (Psalm 139:1–3)

You have searched my heart and you have seen the depths of my darkness. Yet you still chose me. You pursue me every day. You have carried me, married me, and was with me when I buried half of me. It was you I saw in the determined eyes of my groom, and it was you who grabbed my hand when my husband released mine. You are love. Your faithfulness is my hope. With a heavy heart and a happy heart, I will praise you for giving me this journey. It is an honor to follow you as my King.

> *If I speak in the tongues of men and of angels, but have not love, I am a noisy gong or a clanging cymbal. And if I have prophetic powers, and understand all mysteries and all knowledge, and if I have all faith, so as to remove mountains, but have not love, I am nothing. If I give away all I have, and if I deliver up my body to be burned, but have not love, I gain nothing...So now faith, hope, and love abide, these three; but the greatest of these is love.* (1 Corinthians 13:1–3,13)

I Don't Like My Story

There are so many times I looked at the pages you wrote of my story and tried to correct your mistakes. I grimaced when you'd lift your pen, because surely the new plot you were sketching would break my heart again.

But here I am, humbled by your beauty and your grace. For you did not drop your pen when I thought my story was at its end. You continued to write when I didn't want to hear another one of your words in my story. But because of your authorship through my pain, I know hope like a brother and grace like a friend. I am beginning to realize this isn't my story. This story is yours.

Today I looked up at the sky and saw the shade of blue you painted Jordan's eyes. And I smiled. Because I think you planned that just for me.

Lord, thank you for my story.

Nothing penned by your careful hands is an accident. You crafted my story in every detail and you are still writing my chapters.

To the Lord, who is the author and finisher of my faith, please be my author forever. I can't wait to see what is in store in the pages to come!

Therefore, since we are surrounded by so great a cloud of witnesses, let us also lay aside every weight, and sin which clings so closely, and let us run with endurance the race that is set before us, looking to Jesus, the founder and perfecter of our faith, who for the joy that was set before him endured the cross, despising the shame, and is seated at the right hand of the throne of God. (Hebrews 12:1,2)

A QUICK REFERENCE OF
BIBLE VERSES IN TIMES OF NEED

I am afraid to go to sleep:

If you lie down, you will not be afraid; when you lie down, your sleep will be sweet. Do not be afraid of sudden terror or of the ruin of the wicked, when it comes, for the LORD will be your confidence and will keep your foot from being caught.

(Proverbs 3:24–26)

I feel rejected:

For you are the God in whom I take refuge; why have you rejected me? Why do I go about mourning because of the oppression of the enemy? Send out your light and your truth; let them lead me; let them bring me to your holy hill and to your dwelling!

(Psalm 43:2,3)

I feel like no one hears me:

"Call to me and I will answer you, and will tell you great and hidden things that you have not known."

(Jeremiah 33:3)

Behold, the LORD's hand is not shortened, that it cannot save, or his ear dull, that it cannot hear.

(Isaiah 59:1)

I do not know what to pray for:

Likewise the Spirit helps us in our weakness. For we do not know what to pray for as we ought, but the Spirit himself intercedes for us with groanings too deep for words. And he who searches hearts knows what is the mind of the Spirit, because the Spirit intercedes for the saints according to the will of God. And we know that for those who love God all things work together for good, for those who are called according to his purpose.

(Romans 8:26–28)

I feel powerless:

"He shall pass through the sea of troubles and strike down the waves of the sea..."

(Zechariah 10:11)

Who will fight for me now?

"He executes justice for the fatherless and the widow, and loves the sojourner, giving him food and clothing."

(Deuteronomy 10:18)

I want healing from my suffering:

Is anyone among you suffering? Let him pray. Is anyone cheerful? Let him sing praise. Is anyone among you sick? Let him call for the elders of the church, and let them pray over him, anointing him with oil in the name of the Lord. And the prayer of faith will save the one who is sick, and the Lord will raise him up. And if he has committed sins, he will be forgiven. (James 5:13–15)

I feel like I have been left behind:

But the Lord is faithful. He will establish you and guard you against the evil one. And we have confidence in the Lord about you, that you are doing and will do the things that we command. May the Lord direct your hearts to the love of God and to the steadfastness of Christ. (2 Thessalonians 3:3–5)

I feel frustrated that I am still grieving:

"They shall come and sing aloud on the height of Zion, and they shall be radiant over the goodness of the Lord, over the grain, the wine, and the oil, and over the young of the flock and the herd; their life shall be like a watered garden, and they shall languish no more. Then shall the young women rejoice in the dance, and the young men and the old shall be merry. I will turn their mourning into joy; I will comfort them, and give them gladness for sorrow. I will feast the soul of the priests with abundance, and my people shall be satisfied with my goodness, declares the Lord." (Jeremiah 31:12–14)

I am struggling with anger:

Refrain from anger, and forsake wrath! Fret not yourself; it tends only to evil. For the evildoers shall be cut off, but those who wait for the Lord shall inherit the land. (Psalm 37:8,9)

I am struggling with condemnation:

By this we shall know that we are of the truth and reassure our heart before him; for whenever our heart condemns us, God is greater than our heart, and he knows everything. (1 John 3:20)

I am worried about some legalities/gossip about me:

Fret not yourself because of evildoers; be not envious of wrongdoers! For they will soon fade like the grass and wither like the green herb. (Psalm 37:1,2)

Commit your way to the Lord; trust in him, and he will act. He will bring forth your righteousness as the light, and your justice as the noonday. (Psalm 37:5,6)

Will God bring justice to my situation?

Once God has spoken; twice have I heard this: that power belongs to God, and that to you, O Lord, belongs steadfast love. For you will render to a man according to his work. (Psalm 62:11,12)

"The Rock, his work is perfect, for all his ways are justice. A God of faithfulness and without iniquity, just and upright is he." (Deuteronomy 32:4)

I am struggling with panic attacks:

"For I, the LORD your God, hold your right hand; it is I who say to you, 'Fear not, I am the one who helps you.'" (Isaiah 41:13)

I am afraid of death:

O you who love the LORD, hate evil! He preserves the lives of his saints; he delivers them from the hand of the wicked. (Psalm 97:10)

But, as it is written, "What no eye has seen, nor ear heard, nor the heart of man imagined, what God has prepared for those who love him"—these things God has revealed to us through the Spirit. For the Spirit searches everything, even the depths of God. (1 Corinthians 2:9,10)

I am coping through trauma:

But whoever listens to me will dwell secure and will be at ease, without dread of disaster. (Proverbs 1:33)

[Cast] all your anxieties on him, because he cares for you. (1 Peter 5:7)

The LORD is my light and my salvation; whom shall I fear? The LORD is the stronghold of my life; of whom shall I be afraid? (Psalm 27:1)

What is God doing in my life?

I believe that I shall look upon the goodness of the LORD in the land of the living! Wait for the LORD; be strong, and let your heart take courage; wait for the LORD! (Psalm 27:13,14)

I am feeling depressed:

It is the LORD who goes before you. He will be with you; he will not leave you or forsake you. Do not fear or be dismayed. (Deuteronomy 31:8)

There is none like God, O Jeshurun, who rides through the heavens to your help, through the skies in his majesty. The eternal God is your dwelling place, and underneath are the everlasting arms. (Deuteronomy 33:26,27)

For you are my lamp, O LORD, and my God lightens my darkness.

(2 Samuel 22:29)

AFTERWORD

If you have gotten to end of this devotional and are still feeling broken and overwhelmed, I want to encourage you that your story will not end here. The Lord is with you and he will continue to tend to the aches of your heart.

When I began writing these journal entries, I could not even imagine what it would look like to be happy again. I had faith that God could somehow mend my broken heart, I had hope that he would somehow do it, but I could never actually visualize how happiness would ever be my reality. But guess what? He did.

After gently healing my heart and unraveling my unspoken fears, the Lord introduced a strong and gentle man into my life. Little did I know that he would become my real-life Boaz. The way Jon waited for me and pursued me is a love story in and of itself, one I could have never written—only God. He was friends with Jordan in college and the Lord made our paths cross in such a beautiful and redemptive way that I could have never imagined. The Lord used Jon to show me that He wasn't through with me just yet, that my happy ending was just beginning.

I am one of those wives who is 100 percent spoiled by her husband. The life I live now is so sweet and happy that sometimes I wake up with a smile on my face, when I used to wake up with tears on my cheeks. Of course, we still have days when we miss Jordan, but I always have the Word of God to breathe life into my soul and comfort my heart.

Dear reader, know that God isn't through with you yet either. There is more to your life story that he will unfold. Though your next chapters may look different from mine, know that every line is being tenderly penned by your loving heavenly Father. If I can help you on your journey, I'd love to hear from you. You can follow the rest of my story, or share yours with me, at:

cadymorganpatterson.com

Instagram: @cadymorganpatterson

Twitter: @Cady_Patterson

For speaking engagements and inquiries, please email
cadympatterson@gmail.com

BEAUTY FROM ASHES
Donna Sparks

In a transparent and powerful manner, the author reveals how the Lord took her from the ashes of a life devastated by failed relationships and destructive behavior to bring her into a beautiful and powerful relationship with Him. The author encourages others to allow the Lord to do the same for them.

Donna Sparks is an Assemblies of God evangelist who travels widely to speak at women's conferences and retreats. She lives in Tennessee.

www.story-of-grace.com

www.facebook.com/
   donnasparksministries/

www.facebook.com/
   AuthorDonnaSparks/

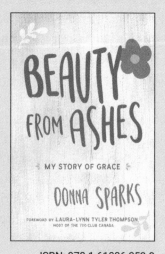

ISBN: 978-1-61036-252-8

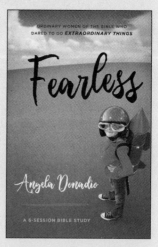